Praise for *It's All in Your Dreams*

"It's All In Your Dreams *is a fun and fabulous addition to any dreamer's bedside table. You'll find simple and powerful techniques for getting 'round the bouncer in the brain who tries to restrict entry to the same old gang of limited and self-limiting thoughts. You'll learn how to look in your dream mirror and see yourself as you really are. You'll discover that, if you are bold enough, you can go to a theater of the mind and rehearse for the life review you'll do after death, and bring clarity from that to make better choices now. Kelly is a spirited ambassador for dreaming, doing essential work in helping to create a dreaming culture in our times. Her energy and humor come crackling off every page."*

> —ROBERT MOSS, bestselling author of *Conscious Dreaming, The Secret History of Dreaming*, and *Dreaming the Soul Back Home*

"For those who use practical tools to study how dreams alter their feelings and aspirations, this book will provide many insights. Kelly Sullivan Walden knows that dreaming is about waking up to a larger life."

> —FRED ALAN WOLF, PhD, aka Dr. Quantum, featured in the movie, *What the Bleep Do We Know!?*, National Book Award-Winning author of *The Dreaming Universe*

"My life has been successful and more powerful by doing dreamwork.... For a profound level of healing, empowerment, and life-changing guidance our dreams offer the guidance our soul is truly hungering for. Kelly Sullivan Walden's It's All In Your Dreams *is a refreshing new look at the power of your dreams.*"

> —LYNN ANDREWS, New York Times bestselling author of the Medicine Woman book series

It's All in Your
DREAMS

It's All in Your
DREAMS

*How to Interpret Your Sleeping Dreams to
Make Your Waking Dreams Come True*

Kelly Sullivan Walden

Conari Press

First published in 2013 by Conari Press, an imprint of

Red Wheel/Weiser, LLC
With offices at:
665 Third Street, Suite 400
San Francisco, CA 94107
www.redwheelweiser.com

Library of Congress Cataloging-in-Publication Data
Walden, Kelly Sullivan.
   It's all in your dreams : how to interpret your sleeping dreams to make your waking dreams come true / Kelly Sullivan Walden.
      pages cm
   ISBN 978-1-57324-590-6
1. Dream interpretation. I. Title.

   BF1091.W195 2013
   154.6'3—dc23

                                    2013000158

Cover design by *www.levanfisherdesign.com*/Barbara Fisher
Cover image: Chagall. Birthday, 1915. Oil on cardboard, 31¾ × 39¼″ (80.6 × 99.7 cm). Collection of the Museum of Modern Art, NY © 2013 Artists Rights Society (ARS), New York / ADAGP, Paris
Interior by Maureen Forys, Happenstance Type-O-Rama

Printed in the United States of America
VG

10   9   8   7   6   5   4   3   2   1

The paper used in this publication meets the minimum requirements of the American National Standard for Information Sciences—Permanence of Paper for Printed Library Materials Z39.48-1992 (R1997).

To my niece, Noel Sullivan, may the family legacy of dreamwork/ play live on through you . . . inspiring you to awaken to the truth of the amazing being that you are and the incredible life you are here to live.

And to the sleeping giant within all dreamers: May this book and these five portals inspire you to fall in love with your dreams so that you can wake you up to your ability to co-create the life of your dreams!

In the case of dreams, fact is stranger than fiction. In other words, all of the stories and dreams referenced in this book are true. Some of the names, however, have been changed, to protect the dreamer's anonymity.

Contents

Where are the answers you seek?
. . . the guidance you crave?
. . . the healing you desire?
It's all in your dreams.

Introduction

*Though we appear to be sleeping, there is an inner wakeful-
ness that directs the dream . . . that will eventually startle us
back to the truth of who we are.*

RUMI

When you nestle yourself into bed, turn off the bedside
lamp, and close your eyes to your daytime reality, your
"conscious self" goes to sleep. Meanwhile, your "dreaming self"
slips out of the covers and tiptoes upstairs to the attic of your
mind to explore the enchanted realm of dreams.

Within this nocturnal territory you are transported beyond
the ego's five senses to a vast, multidimensional playground of
unlimited possibilities. In the realm of dreams you can peruse
the tale of your past or future, learn a topic of fascination, con-
verse with a departed loved one, study at the feet of a master,
find an answer to a perplexing question, discover the solutions
to a health challenge, or explore the larger story of your life.

All this takes place while you are "asleep." Yet for most
people, by the time the alarm blares and they've guzzled their
morning coffee, the exploration of the vast landscape of their
multidimensional soul is shrugged off as "just a dream." This
"just a dream" scenario can be compared to spellbound lovers
on a ship who profess undying love to one another by moonlight
and then find, in the harsh light of morning, back on dry land,
that the glow is gone. In the swirl of "real world" demands, the

lovers revert to being ordinary, sensible, earthbound mortals, vaguely recalling that something magical transpired on the ocean of their dreams. The experience—so real while it was happening—is now as elusive as wisps of cloud.

But, what if it wasn't "just a dream"?

Many of us 21st-century, fast-paced jet-setters fall prey to placing undue emphasis on the tangible, the text-able, and the three-dimensional while discounting the magical, the mystical, and the multidimensional. We would do well to learn from our ancestors who lived close to the earth and were in sync with the tides, seasons, and realms beyond the ordinary. Our indigenous grandmothers and grandfathers considered the dreamtime to be when they were most "awake." They also believed that a society's mental and psychological health was related to dreaming. The more disconnected from dreams, the more sick and out of balance the society. The more in touch with dreams, the healthier the society.

Unfortunately, most people think

- dreams are unimportant;

- they don't have time to record, share, and/or work with their dreams;

- they've lost touch with their ability to remember their dreams.

But consider this:

- Science tells us we all have three to nine dreams every night and can learn to remember our dreams.

- Dreams (even the unpleasant ones) can become our greatest allies.

- We cannot afford to *not* pay attention to our dreams, if we want to thrive while being alive.

Drama to Phenomena

I've been an active dreamer since I was old enough to say "I had the strangest dream . . ." I've had dreams that have guided, healed, and even saved my life, and I've witnessed countless dream-related miracles in the lives of people I've worked with professionally as a certified clinical hypnotherapist for the past seventeen years. I've had my mind blown more times than I can count by the transformative power of dreams to alter a person's paradigm and, quite literally, heal them—I'll share some of these stories with you in this book. Needless to say, I'm one of those people you could call a dream enthusiast . . . and by the time you reach the end of this book, I hope you will be too.

I believe every challenge is born with a solution. Just as jewelweed grows near poison oak, the remedy, healing, or answer you seek—whether it is related to your health, wealth, relationship, or even climate change—can be found near the scene of the crime (even if the conscious mind doesn't recognize it). When we develop a respect for our nighttime dreams, coupled with a basic level of fluency in (or at least a way to decode) its bizarre "language," we are able to find the jewel (weed) in the rough and reap the rewards therein.

This book is not a passive, leisurely read. In addition to it containing many of my personal dreams, it's an interactive, awakening catalyst with questions for you to contemplate, journaling prompts to inspire soulful writing, guided meditations to alter your consciousness, videos to watch, and action steps to take in your waking life. The intent of this book is to help you bridge the gap between the 3-D and the multi-D, and from the ordinary world of drama to the extraordinary world of phenomena.

Nighttime Dreams versus Daytime Dreams

When people find out I'm in the dream business, the question they ask me is generally, "Which kind of dreams do you mean: the weird nighttime dreams or the Martin Luther King Jr. kind?"

My response to them is "Both."

They will either look at me with a furrowed brow as if I just told them a Zen koan (*"What is the sound of one hand clapping?"*) and begin to search politely for the nearest exit, or they will look as if they've just found an all-you-can-eat-buffet after starving for days in the desert. At that point they confide in me every dream they've ever had along with their entire life story. Which, I love, by the way . . . as long as I don't have a plane to catch.

I find that nighttime dreams and daytime dreams/desires go hand in hand, perhaps because they live on opposite ends of the same spectrum. This is what shamans and indigenous dreaming people believe—that we're always dreaming, whether we are awake or asleep; it's all a dream. This may be why, in the telling of a nighttime dream, secret doorways and hidden passages to the fulfillment of their deepest daytime desires are revealed.

Chapter 1

A Sneak Peek at the Five Portals

Within this book, you will discover secrets to remember your dreams, become fluent in the language of dreams, mine the gold from your dreams, reenter your dreams to transform nightmares into rocket fuel for your soul's evolution, program your dreams, and bring the magic of your nighttime dreams to life in your waking state to fulfill your reason for being alive—and much more.

We are multidimensional beings that, according to the American Hypnosis Association (*www.hypnosis.edu/aha/*), inhabit a mere 12 percent of our mental and spiritual genius and potential. This is because we've made the third dimension (that which we consider to be "real": the tangible, visible, audible, *tasteable*, and *smellable*) king. I believe that what is actually king (or queen, as the case may be) is 100 percent of who you are—all your power, all your talent, all your experience, all your capacities, and all your potentialities, beyond the confines of your five senses. The D.R.E.A.M. formula I share in this book is a simple acronym to assist you to achieve dream mastery via insight into your dreams—the ones you have at night and the ones you have by day.

Portal 1—*D* Is for *Declaration*

What is it that you truly want? Stronger than setting an intention to be a powerful dreamer, a Declaration is a lightening rod of conductivity to energize the law of your being. Within this portal you will discover nighttime rituals to care and feed your dream zone. You will learn to declare to yourself, to the Dream Maker, and to the universe that you *will recall your nighttime dreams*. And so it shall be done.

In your waking life, what is it that you truly desire to explore, manifest, and *become?* The Founding Fathers of America didn't create the *Intention* of Independence; they created the *Declaration* of Independence, and thus a new world was born. In order to make a Declaration, you must search your soul to identify *what it is you truly stand for,* what it is you truly desire at the core of your being. There is nothing frivolous about a Declaration. A Declaration is a laser that slices through vagaries, egocentric pretenses, and societal conditioning—all the way to the gold at the center of your heart. This portal explores the ongoing inquiry inherent within your Declaration, which is the cornerstone of the life of your dreams.

Portal 2—*R* Is for *Remembrance*

If you genuinely desire to benefit from the magic of your nighttime dreams in a conscious way, then it begins, at the very least, with you remembering your dreams. As you begin to awaken after eight hours spent journeying through the multidimensions of your dreamscape, *don't move a muscle!* While remaining in the position you were in while dreaming, allow your first thought upon awakening to be "What was I dreaming?" Deliberately press the rewind button in your mind and replay your dreams at least three times. This portal explores techniques like this and rituals to help you remember your nighttime dreams by learning to transfer them from short-term to long-term memory.

If you genuinely desire to live an awakened life, it helps if you can *remember who you really are,* where you came from, and why you are here. Within this portal you learn to discover your true identity as an infinite spiritual being, powerful beyond measure, and heir to all the blessings this earth has to offer. You explore processes and meet dream guides to assist you in recollecting your core strengths, gifts, and genius. Remembering who you are, thus *valuing* who you are, is another cornerstone to awakening to the life of your dreams.

Portal 3—*E* Is for *Embodiment*

The most important aspect of nighttime dreamwork is the embodiment of the energy, emotion, and/or feeling tone of the dream. Whether or not you remember your dream in vivid detail, recalling the way the dream made you *feel* and the energy it produced is key. Within this portal you explore dream alchemy, dream reentry, sexual dreams, and techniques to assist you in embodying the heightened energy of your dream. These processes are among the most valuable ways to affect quantum-level acceleration in your waking life.

When it comes to manifesting the life of your dreams in your waking life, embodiment of the energy is also essential. Einstein said that time (past, present, and future) is all happening at once. Imagine the way you'd *feel* in the future once everything you desire, decree, and declare is in place. Chapter 5 discusses Portal 3 and explores techniques to embody this energy that creates the outer flowering of an inner reality.

Portal 4—*A* Is for *Activation*

Every nighttime dream requires action in the waking world. For example, your action might simply be to share your dream with your spouse. You might be guided to invest in a new technology that has just gone public. Or, your dream might be prompting you to call a friend to talk them out of boarding an airplane. Within this portal you explore the most common dream types and a cutting-edge dream interpretation formula to assist you in discerning its best "real world" application.

Inspired action that leads to magic and graceful manifestation naturally occurs when your dreams are active and alive within you. Struggling upstream will be a distant dream because within this portal you explore the benefits of "SleepWorking" and "Lucid Living." These navigational tools will support you to powerfully participate in living your dream life.

Portal 5—*M* Is for *Mastermind*

When you tell someone else about your dream, you have the benefit of hearing yourself speak; in the telling, details that might otherwise have been lost forever emerge, and even entire plotlines, previously obscured, pop out from behind a mental corner. You also get to hear feedback about your dreams, offering a different perspective that might have remained elusive. Within this portal you discover insights about how to create a Dream Mastermind Group, dream-sharing etiquette, the Hero's *Dream* Journey, dream transferring, collective dreams, and group dreaming.

As they say in the waking world regarding making dreams come true, "It takes a team to realize a dream." Within this portal are suggestions for creating your own *Dream Mastermind Group*—two or more dreamers who are just as invested in your dreams coming true as you are (and vice versa). When you meet (either virtually or in person) in a space of support and accountability, the wheels of your dreams are greased, manifestation is expedited, and you become magnetic to opportunities that will *three-dimensionally* change your life.

Chapter 2

———— ••• ————

The D-spot

At the center of your being you have the answer; you know who you are and you know what you want.

Lao-tzu

One of my very favorite things to talk about is "The D-spot." Not just because it provokes a reaction from people when they think they've misunderstood me. The D-spot is the nexus, the nectar, the sweet spot of your nighttime *D*reams, daytime *D*esires, and your highest *D*estiny.

If the D-spot still feels elusive, then try this metaphor on for size:

Picture a beautiful single-story house. Now imagine the lower part of the house (basement) is where your nighttime *D*reams reside. This dark, underground basement of your being is where the primitive, primal, unconscious hard drive of your mind's computer lives. This is where your buried treasure, secrets, most valuable inner resources, sacred memories, family traits, past-life hardwiring, and belief systems that go back generations are stored. This is where the primitive, foundational, fundamental aspect of who you are is quite at home.

When you climb the creaky stairs up to the next level, you encounter the main floor of the house and are blinded by the light of your daytime *Desires*. In the living room of your home, all that blings takes center stage and your ego sprawls out and runs the show. This is where your ego makes its vision boards (collages of images that reflect your desires: a better job, greater love life, more wealth, vibrant health, etc.). This "living room" is the 3-D reality referred to as the "real world," where we are primarily motivated by our ego's desire to look good, have the right stuff, be recognized, and—if there's time left over in a day—make our mark on the world.

If you choose to peel yourself away from the allure of your daytime desires and explore the higher aspect of yourself, you tiptoe upstairs to the attic. Just a few feet above the hustle and bustle of daily life is where your highest *Destiny* resides. Calm, cool, and in a perpetual state of meditation is your higher self. Up here in the attic of your being is where you can hear the voice of your higher self and angelic nature. Your higher wisdom whispers and your creativity is sky-high. To get here all you have to do is take a moment to get still and elevate your mind just a few steps above the mundane. The attic is where you know things you have never read in a book; it's when you peer into the level of your highest destiny via premonitions, visions, and higher spiritual encounters.

For most people these three aspects of self are vastly separate from one another . . . except in the case of a major life transition or trauma. During these times of heightened reality—like during a crisis or a major rite of passage such as a wedding, a birth, or death—the barriers between the basement, main floor, and attic evaporate. During these moments we have an expanded experience of being both in this world and not of it. These special moments are worth relishing, and yet I believe they are meant to be ordinary occurrences.

When my beloved Grandma Bishop made her transition from the world of 3-D to the realms beyond this world, I remember having particularly vivid dreams and perceiving things with my eyes in waking life that normally I could not see. I was able to see auras as clear as day. I even recall catching glimpses of "people" that were not embodied (à la Haley Joel Osment's character in *The Sixth Sense* and his famous line, "I see dead people.") For me, this expanded way of perceiving was a gift and something that frightened me at the time, but as I've continued to explore this realm, these kinds of experiences, thankfully, have become more frequent . . . and ordinary.

The D-spot is where all levels of our house converge. When we are in the D-spot, we are awake, and we have the heightened awareness from our nighttime dreams; insight about how to more accurately navigate the fulfillment of our daytime desires; and, most especially, guidance as to how to live in accord with our highest destiny.

I frequently envision a moving staircase (a figure-eight escalator, if you will) that connects all three levels of the house in a moving meditation that empowers us to be as awake and aware as humanly possible. In other words, this is where our *humanness* becomes *luminous* to the degree that we can *be* the light of the world (while maintaining access to our ability to pay our light bill). This is the reason I am fascinated by dreamwork. Not just for its ability to make sense of our wacky dreams, but also for its ability to connect us with our roots and elevate us to our highest essence while nudging us toward greater levels of fulfillment and awakening.

Okay, let's face it: When you are in the D-spot, it can be so ecstatic and enlivening that it feels like the emotional/psychological equivalent of the G-spot!

There's No Business like Soul Business

There's more to why I love dreamwork than the aforementioned. In addition to the precognition aspect, the healing benefits, the opportunities for "through the roof" creativity that can lead to exponential contribution to humankind, the reason I am in the dream business is because I'm actually in the *soul* business. Allow me to clarify.

> *This is the true joy in life: The being used for a purpose recognized by yourself as a mighty one. The being a force of nature, instead of a feverish, selfish little clod of ailments and grievances complaining that the world will not devote itself to making you happy. I am of the opinion that my life belongs to the whole community, and as long as I live, it is my privilege to do for it whatever I can.*
>
> GEORGE BERNARD SHAW

I believe it to be impossible to speak, write, or even think about a nighttime dream without finding yourself smack-dab in the center of your soul. From my experience, there is nothing better, nothing juicier, and nothing more fulfilling or confidence-enhancing than to be a human being living soulfully. Nothing says it better than the story of Cyrano de Bergerac . . .

Cyrano and the Soul

We humans are made of divine stuff. We are a tapestry of flesh, blood, magic, and grace. We are infinite beings having a momentary human experience. I believe our soul, like Cyrano de Bergerac, is the intermediary between our dreams and our ego. In the play by Edmond Rostand, Cyrano is secretly in love with the beautiful Roxane, whom he woos anonymously on behalf of his handsome but tongue-tied friend, Christian, who is not-so-secretly in love with Roxane. As archetypes, these characters portray aspects of our own consciousness:

Christian: the awkward, yet handsome ego; mental process; socially acceptable

Cyrano: the soul/nighttime dream; odd and socially *un*acceptable in that he has an especially large nose representing instinct and ability to sniff out extraordinary levels of truth

Roxane: the object of Cyrano and Christian's desire; that which we are striving to attain; the prize; what motivates us in our daytime human experience

When we try to manifest a dream/desire in the waking world with the gall, brazenness, and bullishness of our ego/mental process (even with its good looks and social acceptability), we might snag the guy or girl of our dreams for a moment, but we will never woo our heart's desires to fall in love with us in a way that is truly satisfying to our soul.

In the *Cyrano de Bergerac* story, Christian resents the fact that he needs Cyrano to woo Roxane. Christian tries to go it alone, and in the process, makes a fool of himself, stumbling, and fumbling his words, much to Roxane's disgust. This scene brilliantly demonstrates the ineffectiveness of the ego alone in its vain attempt to capture what it thinks it needs to be fulfilled in this world. However, when our ego (Christian) does the bidding of our soul (Cyrano), our most noble dreams/desires (Roxane) come down from on high, find us worthy, and magnetically join us in our dance of life.

When we are *out of touch with our dreams,* and thus our soul, we are susceptible to ego-level familial, cultural, or societal pressures that cause us to be tongue-tied and clumsy (not to mention completely repellant) because our attempts at manifesting have little or nothing to do with the authentic nature of who we are and why we are here.

If you saw the movie *The Secret* and were inspired by its promise (harness the Law of Attraction to manifest everything you desire) but disenchanted by your inability to suddenly live the life of your dreams, perhaps you felt a bit like Christian must have felt when he ditched Cyrano: impatient, frustrated, and filled with doubt. Perhaps the secret behind *The Secret* is to make sure your soul is part of the equation of your daytime dream creation—a *big* part. When we endeavor to manifest our dreams/ dream life *while being in league with our nighttime dreams, thus our soul*, we are suddenly brilliant, talented, awake, turned on, and "in the zone." From this place, in my experience, I've seen people become irresistible to the most wonderful people, places, and opportunities. When we are in touch with our dreams, and thus our soul, our radar is turned on and we become resonant with fortuitous circumstances beyond the scope of what our logical, ego-selves could ever concoct.

In Touch with Your Dreams, in Touch with Your Soul

When you are in touch with your dreams, and thus your soul, you become a homing beacon for your deepest desires. When you are in touch with your dreams, and thus your soul, even if you get a flat tire, break a nail, or have a truly challenging experience (like losing a house or a spouse), you carry a deep ease within you and an awareness that, in spite of appearances, all is well. When you are in touch with your dreams, and thus your soul, you are more able to live your life, to hear your intuition, to fulfill your potential, to heed your calling, to explore your unique vein of gold, and to woo your particular "Roxane" as you navigate your unique path of enlightenment. When you are in touch with your dreams, and thus your soul, the holy trinity within you (Cyrano, Christian, and Roxane) walk hand in hand in hand into the sunset of your highest destiny.

My *Dream* for You

I've compiled this book and the dreams contained within it so that, at the very least, you will come to experience your dreams as a powerful conductor for good in your life and thus be inspired to dedicate a few minutes a day to your dreams (*before* guzzling that first cup of tea or coffee). My greatest *dream* for you is that you will take the tools contained within this book and become so engaged, so enthralled, and so in sync with your dreams that you will go down in history as one who carries remnants of the dream world into the waking world and leaves a legacy of true benefit to the entire human race.

> *Again and again some people in the crowd wake up.*
>
> *They have no ground in the crowd and they emerge according to broader laws.*
>
> *They carry strange customs with them, and demand room for bold gestures.*
>
> *The future speaks ruthlessly through them.*
>
> RAINER MARIA RILKE

Lofty? I think not. Perhaps you will be inspired to up the ante of your dreamwork/play when you realize you and your dreams are in good company. In fact, the greatest thinkers, scientists, artists, visionaries, and leaders throughout history were ordinary people like you and me, who happened to have a deep respect for dreams. Because of this respect, these mere mortals became legendary as they shaped the world through their contributions to art, science, technology, politics, and spirituality. Many of these people attributed their greatest successes to their ability to carry their dream wisdom and visions across the divide into the three-dimensionality of the waking world.

Consider the following examples:

- Our Founding Fathers, **Thomas Jefferson** and **John Adams,** attributed the philosophy contained within the **Declaration of Independence** to their dreams.

- **Albert Einstein** ascribed the theory of relativity to a dream he had as a young boy.

- **Thomas Edison** dreamed of an electricity-powered lamp. It took thousands of "failures" to put his dream into action, but eventually his dream came to pass, and we use electric light bulbs all the time. (Hopefully this factoid will keep you from complaining next time you receive your "Edison bill"!)

- Colonel Harold Dickson made history's **biggest oil discovery** (which later became the Kuwait Oil Company) based on guidance illumined in his dream.

- Elias Howe sourced his invention of the **sewing machine** to his dreams.

- Dr. Frederick Banting discovered **insulin** in his dream— and won a **Nobel Prize.**

- **Mary Shelley's** *Frankenstein* was inspired by her dream/ nightmare.

- A dream led Otto Loewi to a **Nobel Prize** for his **contribution to medicine.**

- **Dmitry Mendeleyev** beheld the complete **periodic table** in his dream.

- **Stravinsky, Wagner,** and **Beethoven** heard musical compositions, from fragments to entire canons, in their dreams.

- **Bob Dylan** composed music from his dreams.

- **Paul McCartney** praised his dreams for his multiplatinum song **"Yesterday."**

- At the beginning of the dot-com craze, entrepreneur **Jeff Taylor** dreamed his "monster" of an idea in the form of the online employment bulletin board website, *Monster.com.*

- The movie *Avatar* was dreamed in vivid detail by director **James Cameron.**

- The *Twilight* series was dreamed by stay-at-home-mom **Stephenie Meyer.**
- And the list goes on . . .

Perhaps the dream you have tonight will be your break-through to heal your body, solve your problems, lead you to your very own gold mine, or contribute your unique gift to the world. And if your dream "awakens" you, in any way, shape, or form, to the realization of the heroic, beautiful, genius being you truly are, then know you are contributing not only to peace on the planet but also to helping me to sleep (and dream) tonight with a smile on my face.

> *If I can stop one heart from breaking,*
> *I shall not live in vain;*
> *If I can ease one life the aching,*
> *Or cool one pain,*
> *Or help one fainting robin,*
> *Unto his nest again,*
> *I shall not live in vain.*

EMILY DICKINSON

Chapter 3

Portal 1—
D Is for *Declaration*

It doesn't interest me what you do for a living. I want to know what you ache for and if you dare to dream of meeting your heart's longing.

ORIAH MOUNTAIN DREAMER

Declaration: A positive, explicit, or formal statement; proclamation, something that is announced, or avowed; a document embodying or displaying an announcement or proclamation; a law, a statement made to an official.[1]

Intention versus Declaration

You don't get the title "Founding Father" if you're just a pragmatist. Most people know John Adams and Thomas Jefferson were dreamers (visionaries), but what most people don't know is that they were both intensely fascinated with their *nighttime dreams* as well. As Robert Moss writes in his book *The Secret History of Dreaming,* after Adams left the White House, Dr. Benjamin Rush posed a "dream for dream" challenge, whereby Adams and Rush would mail their dreams to one another on a regular basis. The incredible dream-swapping that followed demonstrated how dreams guided both men's thinking on many political issues (including preparing Adams for the consequences of the French Revolution, where he dreamed he was in front of the palace of Versailles, trying to lecture on the requirements for a civilized democracy as a mob of beasts tried to tear him limb from limb). Eventually this dream correspondence included Jefferson as well. It could be said that the most important dream Adams wrote to Jefferson about was a dream he had regarding a "future history of the United States." This dream reflects the language Jefferson penned in the Declaration of Independence:

> When in the Course of human events, it becomes necessary for one people to dissolve the political bands which have connected them with another, and to assume among the powers of the earth, the separate and equal station to which the Laws of Nature and of Nature's God entitle them, a decent respect to the opinions of mankind requires that they should declare the causes which impel them to the separation. We hold these truths to be self-evident, that all men are created equal, that they are endowed by their Creator with certain unalienable Rights, that among these are Life, Liberty and the pursuit of Happiness. . . .[2]

For the last couple of decades, *intention* has been the hot word. When I wanted to meet the man of my dreams, I set an *intention*. When I wanted to lose weight and improve my diet, I set an *intention*. When I wanted to improve my dream recall, before going to sleep I set the *intention*. Intentions are good, don't get me wrong, and they sometimes work. However, I believe Declaration is the new intention. Let's face it: A *Declaration* is an intention on steroids. If you are reading this passage, then I assume it is safe to say you have an interest in up leveling your participation in your dreamwork/play. If that's the case, before you go to sleep tonight, write a Dream *Declaration* that says, "I declare that when I wake up in the morning, I will recall a dream." And watch what happens! As I mentioned earlier, the Founding Fathers of America didn't create the *Intention of Independence*, the *Hope of Independence*, or the *Wouldn't It Be Great If There Would Be Independence*. These great men knew that a Declaration was more powerful than hope, and it operates on a causal level of creation. They created the *Declaration of Independence*, and look at what happened. If it's good enough for them, it's good enough for me!

> *In the measurement world, we set a goal and strive to achieve it. In the universe of possibility, we set the context and let life unfold.*
> Rosamund Stone Zander and Benjamin Zander,
> *The Art of Possibility*

You can also take your Declaration proclamations into the realm of your waking life. It seems to be that when there is a breakdown, a breakup, a breakout—in other words, when things fall apart—we become intensely clear about what we *don't* want. Most of us leave it at that. However, those of us in the know understand that breakdowns of any kind, besides being annoying and sometimes downright painful, provide us with the contrast that leads to the clarity of what we *do* want. We certainly don't have to wait for a breakdown to have this kind of clarity, but we might as well, when they show up, create a great Declaration out of it. This is when the magic happens . . . it's as if all your angels and the entire universe is waiting for your crystal-clear marching orders about what it is you truly want to create in your life, to manifest, and to become, in order to get to work to orchestrate the heavens in your favor.

A while ago, my husband, Dana, and I were going through a really rocky patch. For about two weeks we were on each other's nerves, bickering, and truly bringing out each other's worst (the gift we give each other when we feel safe enough in love to let our most shadowy sides out of the closet). My heart felt as if it were in a meat grinder. Ouch! Yuck! Help!

I'd love you unconditionally, if . . .

LISA-CATHERINE COHEN

One night, as I was going to sleep, I decided to practice what I preach (what a novel idea!) and set a Dream Declaration to come to my rescue. It started off like this:

> "Dream Maker, God, Guardian Angels, Whoever is listening, please bring me some relief, guidance, or a fresh perspective to help me get through this debacle."

I tossed and turned until some banshee part of me screeched (with my inside voice), *"Screw that! I want a miracle! I don't just want insight, a nudge, or yet another action step! I want a f#*%@ miracle! Shake me out like a rug and . . . fix this! You know what I mean . . . and you know what to do. Amen and good night!"*

With that, I fell deeply into sleep. I woke up remembering the following dream:

> Dana is a little boy, about five years old. I observe how cute, innocent, and magical he is as he plays with his toys. Out of nowhere, from behind me I hear a voice sternly reprimand, "Why not try loving him?!"
>
> I respond, "You mean 'Love him' even though he doesn't necessarily deserve it?"
>
> Just loving him was a very different approach than what I'd been doing. I had been miserly squeaking out love to him in dribs and drabs based on what I deemed his loveable behavior . . . and the more I kept score, the more he was going down in flames.
>
> The voice was firm: "Just try loving him!"
>
> "Okay, I can do that, if that is really my marching orders, I can do that."

It was as if all I needed was a little permission to drop the scoreboard, open love's floodgates, and let it rip. So I did . . . and it felt good, healing, and euphoric.

When I awoke the next morning, my heart felt soft, open, and warm for the first time in weeks. I rolled over and saw a smile on Dana's face . . . he resembled that five-year-old boy I'd met in my dream. As we went about our day, and in the days that followed, something unspoken changed between us. I didn't feel the need to poke and prod at exactly how it happened . . . I was just saturated with gratitude that out of seemingly nowhere, we were recalibrated . . . and I have my dream and my Dream Declaration to thank for it.

You certainly don't have to wait until you are in the midst of a crisis to set a great Dream Declaration. On an ordinary day (or night before going to bed) you can follow the guidance of my friend Felix Wolf, author of *The Art of Navigation* (*www.theartofnavigation.com*) and apprentice of the late Carlos Castaneda. He says, "Before you go to bed, instead of telling life what you want, ask life what it wants from you."

Asking the question, "What does life want from me?" is a great way of sidestepping the ego's smokescreen that might confuse you into thinking you desire what society tells you to want. When you line up your daytime desires with the energy that dreamed you into existence, and wrap your Declaration around that, the *Good Orderly Direction* of the universe kicks in and your higher purpose suddenly and swiftly begins to take form.

As a way to prime the pump of your Dream Declaration, I suggest contemplating all the things that bring you joy. I created a Pinterest account (*http://pinterest.com/kellyswalden/stuff-i-love/*) and sometimes I look at my "Stuff I Love" folder before going to sleep.

I Declare I Will Have an Extraordinary Relationship!

The secret to happiness is to put the burden of proof on unhappiness.

ROBERT BRAULT

When Anne came to see me she had been living with her boyfriend, Wayne, for over two years. She was dangling by the hope that at any moment Wayne would propose to her and her life would be complete. It seemed the longer she was in this relationship, the more needy and insecure she was becoming. As you might imagine, this was having a repellant effect on Wayne, driving him to become increasingly more distant. In other words, a perfect storm was brewing.

Anne told me she could feel herself slipping into a self-defeating spiral and needed help to figure out if she should stay committed to this challenging relationship or if she should leave and cut her losses. She was unsure if her feelings of intense low self-esteem were a symptom of her own inner work that needed to be done, or if the relationship itself was adding insult to her already injured self-worth.

Right off the bat I suggested that Anne get to the business of setting some Declarations.

The first Declaration Anne made was to *pay attention to her dreams.* It had been a while since she had paid attention to her dreams and she said, "Maybe my dreams will reveal what's in my blind spot and give me an insight that can help illuminate the truth of my relationship with Wayne."

Second, I suggested she identify her *should*s. You can't heal what you can't feel. So, even though it's not fun, it is always a great idea to give voice to the *should*s that are clamoring in the mind as a means by which to unravel them.

In a quivery voice, Anne spewed:

"I should stay with him because, who am I kidding, I'm no spring chicken . . . he's probably the best guy I could ever hope to be in a relationship with."

"I should stay because he has a stable income, and most people are really struggling right now."

"I should just be quiet about my needs/wants/desires, because if I was less of a high-maintenance girlfriend, he'd probably love me more and want to marry me."

"Who am I to be picky?"

"I should leave because he hasn't asked me to marry him yet. I must look like a complete idiot!"

"What will people think of me if I stay?"

"What will people think if I leave?"

"My mother will be so disappointed in me if I leave!"

"My mother will also be disappointed in me if I stay too much longer without a ring on my finger!"

Once Anne was done quieting the cacophony in her head, I asked her to become clear about what she genuinely wanted in her heart of hearts—beyond her ego, beyond her *shoulds,* beyond her conditioning, and beyond her mother's voice in her head! After a few minutes she began to glow (a telltale sign that someone is in the Declaration Zone).

Anne began to speak in a clear, confident voice (very different than the quivery tone she had just moments before). I asked her to phrase her desires in terms of a Declaration. She nodded, took a deep breath, and spoke with the authority of a Supreme Court judge:

"I declare I will have an extraordinary relationship!"

I could have sworn I heard angels singing. I applauded her for the courage it took to dig deep into her own soul to set her Declaration based on what her soul truly desired. I then asked her to set a "bridge Declaration" (one that could help her connect the dots between where she was at that moment and where she wanted to be).

After a few minutes of contemplating, she spoke in that same clear voice, "I declare within the next six months *I will receive an undeniable sign (either via a nighttime dream or a sign in waking life) that will let me know if an extraordinary relationship is possible with Wayne.*"

Anne's Declarations:

1. I will remember my dreams.

2. I will have an extraordinary relationship.

3. Within six months, I will know with certainty whether to stay or leave my relationship.

A week later Anne showed up for her next appointment with me doubled over in tears. "I got my sign!" she sobbed. "I had a dream the day after our last session that Wayne and I were in a hotel, and I crawled into bed only to find another woman under the sheets. In my dream, Wayne wasn't even apologetic. I woke up very upset and shared the dream with him, to which he smirked coldly, 'Well, what's your problem? You should have gone along with it!'"

Anne expressed to me that she felt slapped across the face and thought, "This is not the way someone in an extraordinary relationship would respond to this situation. My partner in an extraordinary relationship would comfort and reassure me—not rub salt in my wound!"

Several more instances like that happened within the week, leaving Anne with the clarity she declared she would have. As luck would have it, Wayne went out of town for a few weeks on business. During this time Anne found a beautiful apartment, and by the end of the month, without fanfare, she parted company with Wayne.

Within a couple months of getting settled into her new place, Anne shared with me that an old flame came to take her to dinner.

"Regardless of whether or not he is Mr. Right, the friendship we are rekindling is truly extraordinary. There is depth to our communication, mutual respect, listening, eye contact—what a concept—and I feel my confidence coming back," she said with a glow (a telltale sign someone is connected to their D-spot). "This Declaration business really works," Anne said. "It's kind of spooky . . . like magic . . . witchcraft."

"I like to call it *dreamcraft*," I corrected.

Until one is committed, there is hesitancy, the chance to draw back—concerning all acts of initiative and creation. There is one elementary truth that ignorance of which kills countless ideas and splendid plans: that the moment one definitely commits oneself, then Providence moves too. All sorts of things occur to help one that would never otherwise have occurred. A whole stream of events issues from the decision, raising in one's favor all manner of unforeseen incidents and meetings and material assistance, which no man could have dreamed would have come his way.

JOHANN WOLFGANG VON GOETHE

When to Hold 'Em and When to Fold 'Em: Knowing Your Part of the Manifestation Equation

There is much in life that is *not* under our control. And that is a good thing. Our breathing, our blood flow, and the foreign economy are usually things that are not on our "to do" list. If we were wise, we would endeavor to keep it that way and steer clear of vain attempts to micromanage every minute detail in our lives. Janet and Chris Attwood, authors of *The Passion Test*, say, "What can I do today to resign as general manager of the universe so I can allow what I am supposed to be doing?"

The million-dollar question then is, What part *is* under our control? What part of the equation of creating our dream life is up to us? With clarity about what part is clearly ours to play, all we need is the courage, discipline, or willingness to do our part.

The good news is, when it comes to manifesting our Declarations, if we set it up correctly, 90 percent of the work is done. The creator, the Dream Maker, God, the universe, our higher consciousness (or whatever word or phrase works best for you) is *dreaming* us. All we have to do is get out of the way and play our part. What if only 10 percent of the equation is actually up to us? Okay, there's a lot contained within that 10 percent; however it is entirely doable. Think of a surfer. It's not a surfer's job to control the ocean waves. However, it is a surfer's job to practice, get wet, show up, and develop the musculature and intuition to ride the waves.

God, grant me the serenity to accept the things I cannot change, the courage to change the things I can, and the wisdom to know the difference.

REINHOLD NIEBUHR

For us dreamy soul surfers, most of the 10 percent that is our domain takes place during the precious moments bookending our sleep. I consider those moments to be prime real estate, something worth protecting, nurturing, and honoring, because it is the bedrock on which you set your Dream Declarations and thus build the life of your dreams.

During these prime real estate moments—immediately before we fall asleep and directly upon awakening—when the veil between worlds is naturally thin—we can actually set ourselves up to have sweet dreams, remember those sweet dreams (more about dream recollection in the next Portal), and carry that sweetness to the shore of our waking life. When we do this, we have the opportunity to connect to the *big* picture of who we are and why we are alive. Filled with confidence, we can hold our heads high as we make our Declarations, maneuvering through the ocean of our emotion with grace.

Sound simple enough? Well, as they say in twelve-step programs, "It works, if you work it." In fact, at first most of our work is in getting out of our own way and releasing our ten thousand tentacles of attachments to the *should*s in our lives. I've found that when we do our part, and allow the universe to do its part, we have a recipe for deep ease, success, and serenity, no matter what is going on in our lives.

Feng Shui Your Dream Zone

Part of the 10 percent you can do to set the stage to engage powerfully in your Declaration has to do with your physical surroundings. When you sleep you are in the most vulnerable, suggestible state of being that you are in all day. When you *feng shui* your dream zone, you clear the space so that your Declaration can be seen, heard, and felt. Arranging your dream zone in such a way that it becomes a true sanctuary is one of the easiest things you can do to positively affect your sleep and thus your dreams.

> *There are absolutely no worldly circumstances under which you can't or shouldn't be making the very best of things.*
> TUT (Mike Dooley)

Don't worry! This can be done with just a few simple adjustments. As my friend Marie Diamond (*www.mariediamond. com*), the world-famous feng shui expert featured in the movie *The Secret*, says, "33 percent of our experience is affected by our physical surroundings. It is a lot easier to move a desk from one corner of your office to another than it is to change your mental programming."

According to the ancient Chinese system of feng shui, a dream sanctuary is one in which there is a harmonious flow of nourishing and sensual energy. It lures you in while evoking a peaceful feeling tone of joyous well-being. In a dream sanctuary you feel nurtured, replenished, and safe enough to let your guard down all the way, whether for a catnap, a full night's sleep, or for passion beneath the sheets. To create a dream sanctuary, let your five senses guide you as you use the following simple feng shui tips:

Sight

- To ensure a nourishing flow of energy, make sure your bed is in the commanding position in your room (an indirect view of the bedroom door from a reclining position where you sleep) and can easily be approached from both sides.

- For a sense of safety and deep ease, ensure there isn't anything heavy hanging on the wall over your head or on the wall behind you while you sleep (i.e., a large mirror, framed piece of art, or hanging plant.) If there is, make sure to relocate it.

- To support a peaceful feeling of relaxation, remove any electronic appliances (such as a TV, stereo, workout equipment, or computers). If you must have them in the bedroom, then cover them with a swatch of attractive fabric or a room divider when not in use.

- To promote balance, have nightstands or small tables on either side of the bed.

- For a sense of calm and order, keep the bedroom doors closed at night as well as the doors to an adjoining bathroom, closets, and drawers.

- To create a warm, sensual environment, dim lighting in the bedroom or use candles to create a dreamy, inviting mood. If possible use a dimmer switch to adjust the glow.

- To achieve a sense of balance, use soothing colors in your bedroom, such as skin tones to achieve a feeling of peace and calm. These colors range from pale white to rich chocolate brown—whichever feels most soothing, nourishing, and/or nurturing to you.

Sound

- To block out jarring or distracting sounds that might interrupt your dreams or your sleep, I recommend that you create white noise, such as with a fan or air purifier.

- To empower you on a conscious and subconscious level, if you feel that you must listen to the radio or watch a television program as you settle in to sleep, make sure that it is calming and empowering. Remember, the moments before you fall asleep are prime real estate. The words you hear and the sounds you take in as you drift off to sleep are very important and influential to your dreams (and the hard drive of your mind's computer).

Smell

- To keep fresh air flowing in your dream sanctuary, open the windows and draw the shades during the day. If you are unable to open the windows, then get an air purifier to keep the air fresh. According to scientist Boris Stuck from University Hospital Mannheim in Germany, the quality of air in your bedroom is very important and has a great deal to do with your ability to have sweet dreams or not.

- For a pleasant scent in the air, use essential oils and (non-toxic) candles.

- To enhance sweet dreams, lavender, jasmine, and mugwort aromatherapy or potpourri stimulate the mind/body connection and reduce stress levels, thereby releasing positive energy and healing.

Touch

- For a secure feeling as you sleep, make sure your bed has a good mattress, with a solid headboard and high-quality sheets from natural fibers that feel soft, fuzzy, or silky to the touch.

- To promote maximum comfort, adjust the temperature in the room (with additional blankets if it tends to be chilly or a fan if it tends to be too warm or stuffy) to make sure the air temperature is just right for you.

Taste

- To keep your breath as fresh as possible, make sure to brush your teeth before bedtime and use mouthwash if you get up in the night—especially after a midnight snack. If possible, stay away from drinking fruit juice in the middle of the night, as the sugar creates an unpleasant aftertaste that will affect your dreams.

- To quench your thirst in the middle of the night, make sure to have a glass or bottle of water at your bedside.

Dream Declaration Meditation

No trumpets sound when the important decisions of our life are made. Destiny is made known silently.

AGNES DE MILLE

This meditation can be done anytime during the day but tends to be most effective in the moments bookending your sleep (right before sleep and upon awakening—after you write your dreams down in your dream journal). To reap the benefits of this meditation I recommend you access it in any of the following ways:

- Read the Dream Declaration Meditation in a meditative way, slowly contemplating each sentence, breathing deeply with each thought, pausing to close your eyes to take in each element that resonates with you.

- Record yourself reading the Dream Declaration Meditation (slowly, allowing plenty of pauses between the phrases). Play your recording for yourself to enjoy in a relaxed environment with your eyes closed.

- Download the mp3 of this meditation from *www .KellySullivanWalden.com/meditations*

- Create a relaxed atmosphere for yourself where you won't be interrupted.

- Keep a journal and pen nearby to write down your Declaration, as well as any *aha*s or insights stimulated by the meditation.

Begin by taking a deep breath. Allow every breath to be like wind moving the clouds, gently dissolving and removing any and all doubts, confusion, should, *limitations, programming, or conditioning. Imagine with these next few deep breaths you are moving beyond the clouds to the very center of your being.*

With this next deep breath, drop beneath the layers of what you think you're supposed to know, what you think you're supposed to have, and what you think you're supposed to be.

And now, as you move beyond all that conditioning, feel or imagine that you are joyously free-falling to the core of your being.

With this next deep breath, discover you have arrived in front of the golden door of your heart. As this door opens wide, you are invited in. Feel the relief . . . feel that you are home at last. You are surrounded by all the love, support, illumination, and fulfillment you have always dreamed, desired, or prayed for. Feel that in this moment, you are perfect just as you are. Spend a few moments acclimating here, being recalibrated and reunited with your true self.

From this deeply centered place of unconditional love and acceptance, you are now awake with a capital A. From this awake place at the center of your soul, the center of your dreams, the center of yourself, you are in a perfect position to create your Declaration.

From the overflow of your being (not from knee-jerk reacting to the demands of the world, not from lack and limitation, but from the purest place of heart and soul), from the place of your original intention for incarnating in this dimension, open to your Declaration. For example, instead of thinking about what you want from life, become open to what life wants from you.

From this place of effortless connection to the nature of your being, contemplate the qualities with which your core essence is aligned and thus scheduled to experience and express (i.e., bliss, contentment, ease, grace, fulfillment, joy, serenity, surrender, empowerment).

What is it that life would most desire to create through you in your life?

What is it that life would most abundantly want you to have?

(Take a few minutes to marinate in these questions.)

In order to develop an awakened life that sustains beyond a blissful blip on the radar, being in league with your nighttime dreams is key. Declare to yourself, to the universe and to all who hear you:

"I declare that I have excellent dream recall! I am paying attention! I will have vivid dreams . . . dreams I will remember upon awakening . . . dreams that will, in the understanding of them, amplify my ability to Wake Up and be the light in this world that I came here to be!"

And now, while maintaining connection to the center of your heart and soul, identify your Declaration(s). For example:

"I declare I have extraordinary relationships."

"I declare I have a joyous, peaceful life."

"I declare I am healthy and filled with energizing vitality."

"I declare I am well-paid for my talents."

"I declare that my dreams reveal to me how to create my life to be a magical playground that attracts the best people, situations, and circumstances that are perfect for me."

Marinate in this meditation and carry it with you as you drift into dreamland . . . and as you prepare to engage in your active waking life.

Rituals to Enhance Sweet Sleep and Sweet Dreams

The following is a list of a few simple things I've found that can set us up to ensure the most optimal dream/sleep experience possible.

Dream Journal

Think about your bedtime ritual: you brush your teeth, watch TV, read a book, meditate, etc. If you are going to be setting a Declaration and working with your nighttime dreams, then it's time to add one more ritual to this ordinary scene.

- Clear off a corner of your bedside table for your dream journal. If you don't have a journal, *get one!* If you are in a pinch, simply use a yellow legal pad with an ordinary pen (one with a penlight is preferred).

- Write your Declarations in your dream journal.

- Read your Declaration as you drift off to sleep.

- Place your dream journal and pen on your bedside table so that it is *easy* to get to them in the morning when it's time to write down your nighttime dreams.

- When it comes to interpreting your dreams that you've written in your dream journal, refer to the SADDLE formula (discussed in Portal 4—*A* Is for *Activation*, page 163).

Your dream journal is the perfect place for your Declaration to reside. It is also the perfect place to house new Declarations as you continue taking action toward fulfilling your dream life. These simple acts are symbolic of your willingness to do your part of the Declaration manifestation equation (say that ten times fast).

Write Your Declaration as a Bedtime Story

In addition to writing a Declaration, some people find it helpful to switch gears from the logical and mundane to the spectacular and magical, to have a *Declaration Bedtime Story* to read. With your Declaration in mind, write a one-page "story" of your life—the way you see, feel, or imagine it to be if you were living in the highest expression. Here are some questions to prompt your Declaration Bedtime Story:

1. Describe your life when you see, feel, or imagine your Declaration to be fulfilled in your life.

2. What stops (or challenges) you from doing your part of the equation to three-dimensionalize your Declaration? What is the number one thing that stops (or challenges) you?

3. Imagine for a moment that you've overcome your greatest block, obstacle, or challenge to doing your part to usher in your Declaration. Describe who you would be/feel/think/act with this issue behind you.

   - What would be possible for you?

   - How would your life change?

   - What would open up, be different, or be better than it is now?

4. Describe your new "dream self" (you, living your Declaration) in a single word.

5. Describe your new "dream life" in a single word.

6. Write this word in bold letters, calligraphy, or art and place it around your home, office, bathroom, and car, so that in no time you will literally be surrounded in the essence and energy of your dream self as well as your dream life.

7. If you truly embodied your new Declaration, how do you imagine that would impact your business/relationships/health/wealth?

As you read your Dream Declaration Bedtime Story, allow your mind to see, feel, or experience this story as if it were a larger-than-life movie with you in the starring role. Use your *imagic*nation to fill in the details with Technicolor clarity. See the colors, smell the aromas, feel the textures, hear the sounds.

Imagine the ripple effect this fulfilled Declaration will have on your future . . . on the people in your life . . . on the world . . . on the future of this planet . . .

Feel the elation, joy, happiness, and fulfillment of revealing and expressing all your multifaceted radiance, talent, genius, joy, power, spiritual energy, and healing—the fulfillment of your Declaration. Allow these thoughts and sensations to take you by the hand and lead you into dreamland.

As your dreams take their cue from your Declaration Bedtime Story, your subconscious mind is being gently conditioned to accept the elements as normal, natural, comfortable, and safe. As you do this, new neuro-pathways are being constructed in your brain, preparing to help you to embody your Declaration in your waking life. And as an added bonus, as you lie in bed meditating and marinating in this feeling tone, you will soon realize that you are benefiting from your Declaration *before* it manifests in your life.

Sensory Stimulation

Some of the brightest minds of our time have been those that think and feel in a vivid and sensory way: Margaret Mead, Albert Einstein, Martin Luther King Jr., Buckminster Fuller, Eleanor Roosevelt, Picasso, and Rembrandt, to name a few. In order to assist you in bridging dreams into real life, this exercise will expand your mind to make more room for your sensory genius by stimulating your five senses:

Smell

Imagine the smell of freshly baked chocolate chip cookies, cinnamon mulling spices, pine trees, ocean mist, mint leaves, a new car's interior, your favorite perfume . . . and now imagine the fragrance of something you might smell when your Declaration is realized.

Taste

Imagine biting into a juicy, crisp red apple; the taste of warm, buttery mashed potatoes; the minty fresh flavor of having just brushed your teeth; savoring a slice of pecan pie with whipped cream . . . and now imagine what you will eat or taste when your Dream Declaration is realized.

Touch

Imagine petting a fluffy cat, walking barefoot across wet grass, feeling the warmth of a crackling fire on a snowy day, diving into an icy lake on a hot summer day, wearing a warm and fuzzy sweater, dancing wildly to your favorite song . . . and now imagine the texture of something you might feel or touch when your dream Declaration is realized.

Sight

Envision a full moon in a starry sky, a baby's smile, a tangerine sunset at the beach, autumn leaves in all their splendor, looking into the eyes of someone who loves you . . . and now envision what you might see when your Dream Declaration is realized.

Sound

Hear the roar of applause, your favorite musical act playing in an outdoor venue, children's laughter, the ocean breaking against the sand, the crunch of fallen leaves beneath your feet, someone precious to you saying "I love you" . . . and now hear the sound of something you might hear when your Dream Declaration is realized.

Questions for Contemplation

1. Recognize the layers to shed before you can realize your Declaration; for example:

   a. ego

   b. *should*s

   c. comparison to what others have (remember, when you compare, you despair)

   What else do you need to release in order to get to the gold of your Dream Declaration?

2. What is your Declaration for your nighttime dream experience? For example, you might declare:

   a. Upon awakening, I will remember my dreams.

   b. My dreams will help direct me to the answers regarding my

      i. health

      ii. wealth

      iii. relationships

      iv. career direction

      v. creative project

      vi. next steps to take on my spiritual journey

   I, _____,

   (Your name)

   on _____

   (Today's date)

   Declare _____ . . .

3. What is your Declaration for your daytime desire?
   For example, you might declare:

a. Freedom

b. Independence

c. Creativity

d. Healing

e. Deep connected, soulful relationships

f. Rich and unique experiences

g. Wonderment

h. Purpose

i. Fulfillment

I, _____ ,

(Your name)

on _____

(Today's date)

Declare _____ . . .

Whatever you can do, or dream you can do, begin it. Boldness has genius, power, and magic in it. Begin it now.

JOHANN WOLFGANG VON GOETHE

Chapter 4

Portal 2—
R Is for *Remembrance*

The Great Spirit has many ways of communicating with the human being . . . through dreams, imagination, intuition, inspiration, or a hunch. We need to pay attention to our dreams. Don't cast them off as being silly or useless. Be respectful to our dreams and feelings.

WHITE BISON-ELDER

Remembrance: A retained mental impression; memory; the power or faculty of remembering; the length of time over which recollection or memory extends; the state of being remembered; commemoration.

Remembrance and the Castle of Dreams

If you jump too quickly from the dreamtime into your waking life, splash cold water on your face, and guzzle down a cup of coffee, your dreams quickly will become a distant memory . . . and your dreamtime treasures will be left in the dark. Remembering a dream (or even a flittering wisp) is your ticket to play in the game. Without it, you are on the outside looking in.

In order to live lucidly, it is imperative for you to wake up from the illusion of your separation and imperfection and *remember who you really are!* Somewhere tucked away in the recesses of the attic of your mind is the memory that you are beautiful, perfect, magnificent, connected with all life, and here on this planet at this time to shine in the way that only *you* can. Remember? You came here to elevate yourself and everyone around you from the nightmare of separation back to the lucid dream of our immortality and infinite heavenly possibilities. Answer this: How could you possibly live the life of your dreams without this itty-bitty insight? So glad you see my point. If you don't have a remembrance of who you really are, then, by definition, you are sleepwalking through life.

Here's another way of looking at Remembrance from the perspective of dreams: Imagine the realm of your dreams to be an enchanted castle that contains within it a multidimensional world of magic and miracles. There is a moat that separates the castle of your dreams from the mundane world of 3-D reason, rationality, and ordinary reality. When you wake each morning, your dreams deliver you back to your body, gently on the shores of three-dimensionality. For most people, their sojourn to the mystical realm of the multidimensional ends there. However, if you are able to successfully capture at least one dream (or even a dream wisp) before the drawbridge rises, then you will effectively keep the drawbridge lowered throughout your waking state, giving you access to connect with this enchanted realm all day long.

When you wake up too quickly without carrying a trace of your dream with you, you allow the drawbridge to rise, and the actions you take throughout the day tend toward the rational, robotic, logical, and the tried-and-true. Yes, progress can be made, but it can be painfully slow and tedious. However, when the drawbridge is down, your state of being and your actions throughout your day are tethered to the exponential wisdom, compassion, and intelligence from your infinite, extraordinary dreaming mind. It is when the drawbridge is down that quantum leaps take place, awakening happens, and miracles become commonplace. The trick lies in retaining the wisdom gained from the dream and integrating that wisdom in waking life.

> *The returning hero, to complete his adventure, must survive the impact of the world. Many failures attest to the difficulties of this life-affirmative threshold. The first problem of the returning hero is to accept as real, after an experience of the soul-satisfying vision of fulfillment, the passing joys and sorrows, banalities and noisy obscenities of life. Why re-enter such a world? Why attempt to make plausible, or even interesting, to men and women consumed with passion, the experience of transcendental bliss? As dreams that were momentous by night may seem simply silly in the light of day, so the poet and the prophet can discover themselves playing the idiot before a jury of sober eyes. The easy thing is to commit the whole community to the devil and retire again into the heavenly rock dwelling, close the door, and make it fast.*

> JOSEPH CAMPBELL,
> *The Hero with a Thousand Faces*

Persephone and the Pomegranate

It's nearly impossible for me to discuss dreams without bringing up my favorite Greek goddess, Persephone. It may seem like a stretch, but I feel that Persephone's story weaves the perfect context for dream Remembrance and why it is important.

Persephone's story begins like all our stories, in innocence. Envision a beautiful young lass with a flowered wreath in her long flowing hair, smelling the sweet, multicolored flowers, singing lovely songs, twirling, rejoicing, without a care in the world. Persephone (also known as Kore, or "girl" in ancient Greek) is the embodiment of the "maiden" in all her springtime glory.

In her openhearted zest for life, drinking in all the sweetness the world has to offer, she stops to adore the narcissus—the most fragrant flower of them all. Symbolically speaking, this is the moment when she first became self-aware. She discovered the *narc*otic quality within *narc*issism—and we all know what a slippery slope that can be!

At this very moment, the earth opens up beneath her feet, and Hades, God of the underworld, reaches up from his darkness and kidnaps her.

Talk about a nightmare! What a shock for poor Persephone, who, up until this moment, has only known beauty, springtime, and sunlight—to be abducted and initiated into the realm of shadows and darkness. To make things worse, despicable Hades wanted to *marry* her! Can you say *ewww?!* Persephone is out of her element and Hades knows his terrain like the back of his scaly hand. Out of pure survival instinct, Persephone relents to Hades's proposal. Without fanfare, Persephone, who once was the maiden of virtue and innocence, becomes Hades's Queen of the Underworld.

This might seem like a horrible, tragic, and depressing tale except for one tiny thing: adaptation. Oh, yeah . . . and the fact that she is a goddess.

Eventually, Persephone stops running from her power and resisting the mystery within the dream . . . she opens to it . . . explores it . . . and becomes curious and thus knowledgeable about it. After a while, Persephone actually becomes masterful in the Hadean realm. She discovers power she'd never known, revels in secrets about dreams and the unconscious that had been previously unimaginable, and embraces the mysteries and gifts of her own shadow.

Eventually she even grew to love Hades (just as Christine falls in love with the Phantom of the Opera and Belle grew to love the Beast—a genuine respect and bizarre romance form . . . 'tis a tale as old as time.)

As it is with any hero's tale, the moment one becomes comfy and cozy with one stage of the journey, it's a sure sign they are about to be ejected.

Meanwhile, back on earth, the moment Persephone becomes a missing person, Demeter, Mother Goddess of Fertility, turns the earth to ice. It is the world's first winter. As the crops die of frostbite, Demeter raises her staff and demands of Zeus (her husband, father sky . . . the almighty ruler of all gods and goddess)—with the dramatic flair you would expect from a goddess who's just lost her daughter—"Tell Hades to release my daughter or earth will perish!"

With that, Zeus, alpha male God of the universe, commands Hades to return Persephone to the land of the living. Hades balks yet realizes he has no choice, so he acquiesces. However, being the clever God of the Underworld that he is, he feeds Persephone a single pomegranate seed, thus tying her to Hades for a third of every year, ensuring her return to him. This is the story of how our seasons came to be as well as the amount of time we spend asleep.

Apollo shows up on his winged chariot and whisks Persephone up and away from the realm of darkness to the world of sunshine, flowers, and beauty once again. As you might imagine, Persephone was a bit discombobulated—once more cast out of her comfort zone. Back in the sunshine of earth, Persephone is no longer the little girl (Kore) she once was. She struggles for a moment or two or three with the disorientation of yet another identity crisis (kind of like waking up from a wild dream).

Again, this story might seem tragic, if not for Persephone's ability to adapt. She integrates her shadow into her light, and something extraordinary happens: *she becomes a full-blown Goddess (with a capital G) . . . and a force to be reckoned with!*

No longer afraid of her shadow, nor from her light, she walks boldly, fearlessly, and with confidence and true power in both realms. And thus she becomes the ultimate healer/alchemist/dreamer/goddess.

Everyone has a tour of duty in the Hadean realm (a.k.a. a dark night of the soul). However, some people get stuck there for too long. When this happens, according to myth, Persephone has the ability to bring them back to the light. When people need help understanding their depth, their shadow, and their dreams, Persephone is on call to give them a little taste of the underworld.

Thus the goal of dream Remembrance is to stand as Persephone, with one foot in the waking world and one in the nocturnal realm so that we can access both worlds simultaneously. This may sound weird to you. And if it does, then that's okay. *Weird* has its roots in Middle English, when it was spelled *wyrd* and meant "one who can stand in both worlds, thus having the ability to control fate and destiny and to operate supernatural influences." I think *weird* has gotten a bum rap over the years and it needs a new publicity campaign. I think *weird* is the new *cool*, don't you? Persephone and I certainly do!

Dreaming Is Seeing

Dreams are like letters from God. Isn't it time you answered your mail?

MARIE-LOUISE VON FRANZ

I was recently at a gathering and found myself in conversation with a brilliant woman who is a psychic channel. She told me that she pays close attention to her dreams and that she "dreams" all the time. As I was listening to her, I felt as though I gained a glimpse into what she meant by "dreams." I suddenly realized that she was not referring to dreams as being otherworldly phenomena, but simply the perception of that which is already here, however imperceptible to our ordinary logical, linear minds.

In fact, many indigenous cultures, including the ancient Egyptians, knew this. The ancient Egyptian word for dream was *rswt*, which also meant "awakening" with its symbol being the wide-open eye. The ancient Egyptians believed that when we were dreaming, we had the potential to be most awake, and that perception was available 24/7.

With this perhaps we might consider changing the way we relate to dreaming and think of it more as seeing what is right in front of our faces, if we only have the eyes to see. Consider that scientists have proven that human beings are capable of taking in only a fraction of 1 percent of the information that surrounds us. And within that fraction of 1 percent, in our typical waking state we perceive 80 percent based on our past, and only 20 percent of what is actually occurring.

For example, if you go to a party of someone you've never met, you shake hands with the host and immediately tell them, "You remind me of an old college buddy." You look around the house and see a staircase that reminds you of your childhood and hardwood floors that remind you of the ones you have in your house; a burning cinnamon candle reminds you of Christmas; the roasted red pepper and goat cheese salad reminds you of your summer in Greece; and the music playing in the background reminds you of the kind your sister would like. We rarely perceive what is actually happening around us with fresh eyes, which means we only pick up an aspect of it (20 percent) and leave the rest (80 percent) on the table (the table that reminds us of our late grandmother).

This ability to sort through the data that constantly bombards us, categorize it, profile it, discard what we perceive to be irrelevant, and focus on what is valuable is how we have survived. However, what if it was possible, as an ever-evolving species, to operate at our full wattage? What if it was possible to acclimate our awareness toward becoming 100 percent in present tense? Lofty, I know, but, what if? And what if improving our dream remembrance is one of the key exercises we can practice to build the consciousness to get us there?

The following is a story about how a fourteen-year-old girl's nighttime dreams continue to help her and her family access a higher level of awakening.

Bridge Angel

Claire came to see me because she wanted support and confirmation regarding a puzzling series of dreams. When she entered my office, I saw a diminutive fourteen-year-old girl (a miniature Angelina Jolie meets Anne Hathaway). In most regards, Claire is beautiful, charming and vivacious . . . utterly typical of her age. However, Claire is atypical in one important way: Since infancy she has suffered from cystic fibrosis. *Suffered* is perhaps too harsh a word, since aside from the oxygen tank at her side, the tubes running into her nose, and the treatments that include having her lungs vibrated for an hour or two a day, you would scarcely see a difference between Claire and any other bright, precocious, teenage girl.

Being in and out of the hospital is an ordinary part of Claire's life. A year before our meeting she was in a coma with a three-percent chance of survival. Shortly after miraculously reviving from her coma, she had the following dream:

> My best friend, Alicia, and I are walking through a playground and we come across this twisted vine that catches our attention because it reminds us of "Jack and the Beanstalk." When we touch the vine it carries us (at turbo speed) up to the "galaxy." We end up in a place high above the clouds. It is the most magical and beautiful place I've ever seen. Not only is it filled with the most brilliant colors, but it is also filled with the answers to

every question we can think of. For example, Alicia has "boy problems," but up here in the galaxy, she completely understands why the boy she likes doesn't call or text her when he says he will—it all makes perfect sense!

I ask a question I've always wanted to know the answer to: "Why do I have this illness?"

The answer is revealed immediately.

"You've done good work in past lives. Your reward for all the light you have brought to others is the gift of a short life. You won't have to grow old like so many other people. You will get to have a lot of friends, bring joy to many people, make a difference in the world by shining light on cystic fibrosis through your foundation [Claire's Place], and then you get to leave, without having to grow old."

This answer makes me feel so good. I no longer have to think of my illness as a punishment for something I've done wrong or because I'm bad.

We explore the "galaxy" for what seems like months, having the best time ever. Up here I don't need my oxygen tank or my medical treatments at all!

At some point we realize we've been gone for what seems like weeks and we don't want our families back on earth to worry about us, so we travel back down the vine to earth. Luckily, in earth time, we were only gone a few minutes. Whew!

Back on earth we receive a letter telling us that we are "Bridge Angels" who have been given a special mission to find people who have just died and take them to the "galaxy." Most people don't know how to get there on their own, so they need a Bridge Angel to escort them. Since we know how to get there, we are perfect candidates for the job.

Alicia and I are so excited to have such an important assignment . . . especially because we know from personal experience how amazing this place is . . . we can't wait to share it with people!

I have this dream a lot, and so far we have taken hundreds of people to the "galaxy"—all kinds of people, young and old, every ethnicity and religion. They all die in different ways. From the human perspective it all seems so tragic, but when Alicia and I are in Bridge Angel mode, it's like magic. Even though every person we take to the galaxy loves it once they get there, at first they resist us, because they are afraid of leaving their familiar world and loved ones behind . . . and who could blame them?

We have to be very convincing. We found this out the hard way. Once there was a man so stubborn he wouldn't let us take him, so we finally let him go. We found out later that no one could find him because he had apparently gotten "lost." This made us realize the seriousness of our job. Since that moment we have never let another one slip by, no matter how much they kick and scream. In every case, all the people we take to the "galaxy," once they see the beautiful colors and feel how wonderful it is to be there, hug us, thank us for taking them, and walk into the light with smiles on their faces.

Dreams Are Not Just for the Dreamer

Because Claire walks a fine line, in real life, between here and the hereafter, this dream has become a source of peace and reassurance for her and her family—especially her seven-year-old sister, Elly. Each time Claire gets hospitalized (which is frequent), little Elly gets scared and seeks reassurance from Claire. Claire and Elly share a bedroom and sometimes Elly asks Claire to tell her Bridge Angel bedtime stories. These stories reassure Elly and send her to dreamland with a smile on her face:

"Tell me again about the galaxy."

"What is it like to be a Bridge Angel?"

"When I die, will you be my Bridge Angel?"

"Can I come visit you in the galaxy before I die, or do I have to wait till I die?"

"Can we paint pictures of you in the galaxy so I know where you are going to be?"

Ancient dream cultures, such as the Senoi of Malaysia, believe that dreams are not only for the dreamer, but are meant to be shared so that the entire tribe may benefit. This is definitely the case for Claire's "Bridge Angel" dream. When I spoke with Claire's mother, Melissa, she told me that she, too, takes refuge in the dream.

"Claire's dream has been a great gift to me. It gives me a strange comfort in the midst of what would otherwise be unthinkable. In some way it seems this dream is preparing me (us)—like nothing else could—to cope with what would normally be an unbearable situation (having a child with special needs who is frequently hospitalized, and the constant threat of things getting worse) by giving us a positive frame to put around it. One of the reasons for this odd feeling of peace we are able to hold on to is because Claire has embraced death in a powerful way. She is teaching us how to have a positive outlook on death, hers and our own. Because of her dream, Claire sees the afterlife as if it were a fabulous vacation she is preparing to take. She speaks of her dream locale in such vivid detail that we all share the mental imagery of this place, and it feels so real. There is comfort in knowing that if Claire gets there before us, we have a place to meet and be together again."

In the meantime, Claire is in no hurry to die; she is focused on living life to the fullest while she is here and inspiring others to do the same. See for yourself by going to Claire's Facebook page (*www.facebook.com/clairewineland*) and to her foundation's website (*www.clairesplacefoundation.org*). So far she's helped to organize three flash mobs, was a featured speaker at a recent TED Conference, and was the subject of an ABC news special.[3]

The most inspirational thing to me about Claire is that when her mind wanders to thoughts of death or dying, a peaceful smile crosses her face. This is because her dream has revealed to her what a Native American friend of mine has described as one of the greatest secrets: "To be unafraid of death . . . live fully, as if death were right over your shoulder."

And who knows, maybe she really is a Bridge Angel who is actually helping transport newly departed souls to the other side during her dreamtime. All I know is when my time comes, there's no one but Claire I'd want to be my escort to the hereafter!

Remembering Your Dreams and Remembering Who You Are

I believe Claire's dream is important to drive home the core principal of Remembrance for a couple of reasons. For one, it underscores the exponential value of a remembered dream and its effect not only on the dreamer, but also on the entire "tribe."

Secondly, Claire's dream is a powerful message about how important it is to have a Remembrance of who we really are. In the "galaxy" in Claire's dreams, she is filled with a knowing, a sense of peace, joy, and wisdom, because she is reconnected to her true essence as an infinite being. Because of this higher (and truer) awareness, Claire doesn't relate to herself as a victim of a cruel disease, but as a being that has an important mission, who is grateful to be alive, lucky to be who she is, and fortunate to live her life, regardless of how short as it may be. And who knows, with a spirit like hers, she may outlive us all!

The Big Story versus the Little Story

There is a saying, "Many are called, but few answer." We are all being called every day and every night to peek behind the curtains and glimpse the big picture, the higher view, the hero's journey, and remember the Big Story of our lives. Viktor Frankl, the author of *Man's Search for Meaning,* teaches that when we identify with the Big Story of our lives, we recognize that even our greatest challenges can be seen as worthy quests, worthwhile adventures, full of dignity and purpose.

> *Bill Moyers: Do you ever have this sense when you are follow-ing your bliss, as I have at moments, of being helped by hidden hands?*
>
> *Joseph Campbell: All the time. It is miraculous.*
> THE POWER OF MYTH (PBS, 1988)

When we identify with the "little story" (a.k.a. forgetful-ness), the tale is the same for us all: varying degrees of stress, trauma, sadness, rejection, loneliness, pain, frustration, despair, struggle, heartache, loss, and victimhood. From the perspective of the little story, we relate to ourselves as tiny, groveling crea-tures, needy, greedy, and even parasitic in our constant attempt to hoard security, attention, recognition, money, love, fortune, fame, respect, validation, or even just our "daily bread." *Yuck!* From the little story perspective, it's easy to see why, statistically speaking, according to Bob Murray PhD and Alicia Fortinberry (creators of the Uplift Program), more people are depressed in the Western world than ever before.[4] In fact one in ten adults is depressed, and "preschoolers are the fastest-growing market for antidepressants! At least 4 percent of preschoolers—over 1 mil-lion—are clinically depressed." *How depressing is that?!*

However, as a by-product of remembering our dreams, it is possible for us to glimpse the Big Story of why we are alive. When we relate to ourselves (and teach our kids to relate to them-selves) from the perspective of the Big Story (deep breath), we realize we are co-creators in a friendly universe. We see that we are each an unrepeatable phenomenon. We see that, regardless of our temporary struggles, we have won the lottery as evidenced by the miracle of our presence in a physical body here on earth. In fact, consider that the chance of you being born into the body, family, and life that you have is a billion to one. You are a living, breathing, miraculous lottery winner, surrounded by billions of other lottery winners—most of whom have forgotten they are lottery winners!

This next dream story illustrates how a dream can help a person shift perspective from the little story to the Big Story and thus remember who they are and why they're here.

My Interview with George Bailey

In the movie *It's a Wonderful Life,* the main character, George Bailey, played by Jimmy Stewart, is a good guy with a chip on his shoulder. He has big plans for his life that include travel and adventure, fortune and fame, none of which come to pass. His sense of duty and familial obligation prompt him to stay home, postponing his personal fulfillment in order to be of service to others. At a pinnacle moment in the story, George is defeated and disheartened by the realization that the family business is going belly-up and that his family and community would be better off without him. As he prepares to jump off a bridge to end to it all, his guardian angel, Clarence, intervenes. Clarence, a bumbling angel in training, shows George what life would have been like if he had never been born. While wandering throughout this bleak alternative reality, George realizes that his contribution to life made a positive difference in many people's lives. With this new perspective, he utters his famous line: *"I want to live again!"* He is given a second chance at what he now sees as a wonderful life!

On a personal note, I'm the type who *never* watches a movie more than once. However, I've made an exception when it comes to *It's a Wonderful Life.* I've seen it more than twenty times and I cry my eyes out every time! George Bailey is one of my greatest heroes . . . a knight at my inner round table, for sure.

Jimmy Stewart and his George Bailey character figure prominently in a dream of mine:

> I'm in a church parking lot in line to meet Jimmy Stewart. He is in a trailer/mobile home, and is greeting people and shaking their hands. It is my turn to meet him, and like an effusive schoolgirl, I ask him if he would do me the honor of being a guest on my radio show (*The D-Spot*). I prattle on about how, because of the current economic situation, many people are having "George Bailey moments," in that they're losing their homes, wriggling under the thumb of sinister lending institutions, and feeling their dreams have been dashed.

I interpret Jimmy Stewart as a "steward" (messenger) to remind me to show the people having their own "George Bailey moments" the Big Picture of their life. In my dream, George Bailey was in a mobile home, symbolizing the fact that we can bring "home" with us wherever we roam. And where better to park your home than in a church parking lot: a place that symbolizes the intersection of the human becoming aware of their divine nature?

Like Carl Jung, I believe you can view everyone and everything in your dream as an aspect of yourself. In this case, I was shaking hands with the "George Bailey" aspect of myself—to help me remember (and also to remind others) that the *R* in the D.R.E.A.M. formula is not just about *r*emembering nighttime dreams, but also about *r*emembering *who we really are.*

When we are in a state of *Remembrance,* we live lucidly and are awake to whom we are, remembering where we're from, and why we're here. When this happens we are inoculated from the ordinary human drama of stress and struggle, drama and trauma. When we live lucidly, we are lifted to a higher place in consciousness that allows us to be joyous, passionate, and even quite possibly *grateful for our struggles*—as they are the grains of sand in the oyster that create pearl after pearl of wisdom.

Blind Spots: Dreams That Help Us See What Our Conscious Mind Can't

It's never fun to confront our blind spots. When we discover a blind spot, it's as pleasant as finding out you've been walking around with your skirt tucked into your panties. (You too? I'm glad to know I'm not the only one!)

Any way you slice it, discovering a blind spot is just plain old embarrassing to our ego—who likes to think we've got everything figured out—ha! But the truth is, even though we know a lot, all we know could fit on the head of a pin compared to what is knowable in the universe. So, if we are the true Warriors of Awakening we claim to be, we would celebrate each time someone brings to our attention the fact that we have an annoying personality trait, a behavioral tick, or a long strip of toilet paper attached to our stylish high heel.

Luckily for us, our dreams can help us come to terms with some of these blind-spot gremlins and find peace with them so that we don't have to feel annihilated but rather poised to celebrate the next time they are revealed. Here's an example of how my dream helped me reclaim my dignity after the horror of a blind-spot revelation:

> Robin Williams is a lion tamer on trial for his unconventional methods of keeping his lions in check. He is dressed in lion tamer regalia—riding pants, a safari hat, tall black boots, a khaki long-sleeved shirt—and carrying a whip. The dream takes place in a courtroom. The judge and jurors are hostile

toward him, and his case is going down in flames. His shoulders slump as defeat and shame weigh him down. As a last-minute Hail Mary, lion tamer Robin Williams bolts out of his chair, raises his left hand in the air, points his whip toward the heavens, and shrieks, "LULLABALLAHABLALALA!!"

The courtroom was shocked, dumfounded, enraptured, hypnotized, and mesmerized. I heard Robin Williams say to himself, "Apparently the same tactic that works with lions works with humans."

The spellbound courtroom, now the lion tamer's command, proclaimed him innocent. The dream concludes with Robin Williams, the unconventional lion tamer, sauntering out of court with his head held high, smiling, and breathing in his victory.

———————

The next day I went to see a matinee of *Life in a Day* with my husband, Dana, and our friend Ron. The movie brilliantly tells the true story of seven billion people, in 190 countries, in one twenty-four-hour period. As the credits are running at the movie's conclusion and tears are streaming down my face, Ron turns to me and says, "You're a trip to watch a movie with!"

Perplexed, I tilted my head, crinkled my brow, and innocently asked, "What do you mean?"

He guffawed and replied, "You are more vocal than the movie. Next time I'll just watch you instead! It's like you are part of the action."

Dana chimed in with an I-told-you-so look on his face. "Kelly, I've been telling you, but you don't listen . . . and it's getting worse."

I apologize to Dana and Ron, feeling as if I'd been hit by a two-by-four across the forehead. "I had no idea," I lied. I'd been told before that I was a loud listener. "But," I sheepishly tried to defend myself, "Aren't my sounds natural—don't they express what everyone is feeling/thinking/doing—given the circumstances in the movie? I mean, come on, the guy cracks an egg and there's a live chick inside, and he eats it! Didn't everyone scream bloody murder?"

"No," Dana and Ron shake their heads in unison.

"You mean to tell me I was the only one in the movie theater making any noise?"

They nod.

The two-by-four strikes again, this time to my gut. I feel dizzy and an urge to dig a hole beneath all my spilled popcorn.

For the rest of the day, I'm self-conscious about every conversation; I monitor my every sound. I feel as if I'm on trial, and I am guilty as charged.

This triggers my memory of the lion tamer dream from the night before. What might the lion tamer on trial have to do with this blind-spot revelation? Hmm.

I breathe—something I hadn't been doing much of since I was put on trial in the movie theater—and I begin to feel the slight rumblings of an *aha* moment threatening to emerge:

- Astrologically speaking, I am a Leo (the lion). According to astrologers, I am very Leonine (loud, roaring, flamboyant, filling up the space, warm, loyal, and one who is known for *holding court*.)

- I believe every character in our dreams is an aspect of ourselves, which makes Robin Williams, my inner comedian, the tamer of my out-of-control Leonine wildness by using shock to get my attention.

- That same shocking abruptness can silence my inner critic that judged me and might, if left to its own devices, label me as guilty, put me in jail, and throw away the key.

- Perhaps dreamwork, itself, is an unconventional method for self-realization (a.k.a. lion taming).

The feeling of freedom Robin Williams had as he left the courthouse is what I choose to embody. He overcame condemnation and emerged victorious. Instead of beating myself up, I can choose to feel grateful that the universe and everything within it is, indeed, conspiring on behalf of my (our) greatest good, to get me (us) to wake up, become aware of my (our) oddities, and take conscious ownership of the aspects of myself (ourselves) that are unconventional, so that we can have them *without them having us!*

As I sit here today, I feel grateful for the dream and for the awareness. I am actually even excited about the opportunity to excavate other blind spots, with the help of my dreams to soften the blow. And you should know, if you see me at the movies, you might want to sit on the other side of the theater, because I may or may not choose to use my inside voice to express myself!

Saved by the Light

Okay, let's get to the business of *remembering* who we are and why we are here.

Could there be a more important time in history than this to wake up?

Could there be a more important time to dream a new dream for your life?

Could there be a more important time in your personal history than this to remember the truth of who you are?

Dannion Brinkley (*www.dannion.com*) is the author of the *New York Times* Best Seller *Saved by the Light*. Dannion has died three times, come back to tell the tale, and is known affectionately as "Dr. Death." He teaches that we all have a "holographic life review" that happens when we die. He says we all get to experience our lives in vivid detail from an omniscient point of view, from the perspective of the person on the receiving end of our interactions, and through the eyes of someone who unconditionally loves us.

"This process," reports Brinkley, "straightens you right out. It means from that moment you have your life review, if given the opportunity to interact once again as a human, all you will want to do is to be kind, generous, appreciative, and loving to everyone you encounter . . . including yourself."

It is a most mortifying reflection for a man to consider what he has done, compared to what he might have done.
SAMUEL JOHNSON

In a bizarre series of dreams, I repetitively was shown my life review, as if I had died. I was shown real-life scenarios where I had, indeed, chosen the high road. However, most of my life review illumined where I had *not* chosen the highest road and the consequences of my words and actions on the people around me, most of which I had never previously been aware or even considered.

For example, on my first day of junior high school, I was eleven years old, gangly, awkward, feeing too tall, and more than a bit klutzy. It was my great desire to be cool, and I tried with all my might to act as if I were. My attempts to act cool got the attention of a group of older girls, and before I knew it, I was surrounded by a herd of popular eighth-grade girls who called me a series of four-letter words I had never heard before—but I could tell by their faces and body language that it wasn't good.

Shaking and fearing I would throw up, I somehow pulled off the acting role of a lifetime and pretended to be unfazed, sarcastic, and holier than thou. "Really?" I said. "All of you eighth graders are ganging up on one sixth grader. How pathetic.

You must feel really tough. Wow, I'm impressed." With that, I flipped my hair and walked away as if I was God's gift to middle school, and as if those tough girls were nothing more than pesky mosquitoes.

I always marveled at how I handled that moment (and the many other moments that followed). I was impressed at my ability to come up with a coping mechanism for surviving junior high without getting beaten up—by fooling those girls into thinking I was a pit bull when, on the inside, I was a quivering Chihuahua.

However, in my dreamtime life review I saw an entirely different movie possibility. I saw that had I been in a state of Remembrance, plugged in to source, illumined with the awareness of being flooded by all the love in the universe, I would have seen how afraid the "mean girls" actually were beneath *their* bravado. I might have seen how they were, in fact, compensating for their own pain and lack of self-worth. Had I seen this, I might have embraced them and reassured them of their beauty, preciousness, and true identity as one with the divine.

Okay, this might have been a tall order for an eleven-year-old. However, in the realm of infinite possibilities, it was an available option, one I wish I had chosen. I continued reviewing my life from the vantage point of being completely awake. It was quite a different life experience, indeed. When I finally awoke from the last life-review dream in this series, I felt I had lived the last scene from the movie *Groundhog Day*. Feeling inspired, I set a Declaration to live, to the best of my ability, from this moment forward, as awake as possible.

What if we don't have to wait until we die to have a holographic life review? What if we don't have to pray to have a dream wherein we had a life review? What if we didn't have to hit rock bottom and want to jump off a bridge to have our personal "Clarence" divinely intervene to help us remember who we are? Perhaps, if we choose, we can have a life review now. Why not? Why put off till we're on the other side what would benefit us now?

There's nothing in this world that encapsulates the message of how to "awaken" more than the Prayer of Saint Francis. Whenever I've heard this prayer, no matter how asleep I might be, it startles me awake. I hope it startles you back into the remembrance of the truth of who you are—not as a "getter," but as a giver of all that you desire to receive:

> *Lord, make me an instrument of your peace,*
> *where there is hatred, let me sow love;*
> *where there is injury, pardon;*
> *where there is doubt, faith;*
> *where there is despair, hope;*
> *where there is darkness, light;*
> *where there is sadness, joy;*
> *O Divine Master, grant that I may not so much seek to be*
> *consoled as to console;*
> *to be understood as to understand;*
> *to be loved as to love.*
> *For it is in giving that we receive;*
> *it is in pardoning that we are pardoned;*
> *and it is in dying that we are born to eternal life.*

Forget and Forgive

For a moment, take the definitions you normally associate with the words *forgetting* and *forgiving*, and toss them aside. Become open to new definitions.

As I experienced in my Dreamtime Life Review, when I was "sleepwalking" and asleep to who I really was, I related to myself as an "empty bucket," constantly seeking approval, protection, security, love, validation (fill in the blanks). The empty-bucket way of being caused me to be in full-throttle taking, hoarding, protecting, and "getting" mode. In other words, when we relate to ourselves from a state of illusion, of having an empty bucket, then our lives are "for *getting*" (for-getting).

> *When I have forgiven myself and remembered who I am,*
> *I will bless everyone and everything I see.*
>
> A Course in Miracles

Conversely, the *Remembrance* state is a plug for the hole in the bucket. When we are awake and remembering who we truly are, we are in a state of genuine seeing with pure awareness, receiving to the degree that our bucket is overflowing with well-being, abundance, wisdom, and source-energy to share. In a state of Remembrance, our lives are dedicated to service, sharing, gifting, and uplifting. When we *remember* who and what we are, we can't help but share from the overflow of our being, and our lives are "for-*giving*" (for-giving). We realize the more we give, the more we receive. (*Receive,* by the way, comes from the Latin verb *recipere,* which means to regain or take back that which was *ours to begin with*. Receiving, just like remembering, is about reclaiming that which was already ours!

> *When you look without grasping, the whole universe is look-*
> *ing out of your eyes. It's an opportunity to see what it is to*
> *move without a sense of a central "me."*
>
> Mukti

When we are awake, we realize the pure bliss in life is in reminding the people who have "for-gotten" who they are and that they are whole, perfect, complete, and utterly "for-given" (in all aspects of the word). Consider for a moment the traditional meaning of the word forgiveness. Perhaps the only thing to be "for-given" is how we behave when we fall asleep and for-get who we really are. When we are unplugged from our source, just like an appliance that is unplugged, we cannot function as we are designed to. But when we are plugged in, just like a toaster or blender plugged into an electric socket, the electricity begins to surge: the toaster can toast, the blender can blend, and the human can act humane . . . shining, beaming, in the way it was designed.

Life Review Meditation

This meditation can be done anytime during the day but tends to be most effective in the moments bookending your sleep (right before sleep and upon awakening—after you write your dreams down in your dream journal). To reap the benefits of this meditation. I recommend you access it in any of the following ways:

- Read the following in a meditative way, slowly contemplating each sentence, breathing deeply with each thought, pausing to close your eyes to take in each element that resonates with you.

- Record yourself reading the meditation (slowly, allowing plenty of pauses between the phrases). Play your recording for yourself to enjoy in a relaxed environment with your eyes closed.

- Download the mp3 of this meditation from *www .KellySullivanWalden.com/meditations*

- Create a relaxed atmosphere for yourself where you won't be interrupted.

- Keep a journal and pen nearby to write down any *aha*s or insights stimulated by the meditation.

Take a few deep breaths. Release and let go of any cares or concerns. Each breath represents a release and a letting go of all physical form, all impermanence, and all that is tangible. With each new breath, you are embracing the love and light within you and around you. You are embracing all that is permanent, true, and real with a capital R.

As you are breathing deeply, you are rising above your circumstances, rising above your fears, rising above your judgments, rising above all limitations, and rising into a higher realm of consciousness.

As you continue to rise, you find yourself above the clouds of the three-dimensional world, in a place of pure light, love, acceptance, and connectedness with the whole of life. In this place there is no limit to the love, to the possibilities, to the beauty.

You are literally surrounded and enfolded in a realm of infinite potential, infinite possibilities, infinite love, expansion, and goodness. It is in this place that you find your way to a comfortable place in the Life Review Theater, and enjoy the show . . .

The screen at first is dark . . .but soon you will notice a speck of light. Notice how this light grows larger and larger, filling the entire screen. And now, as your eyes adjust, from an omniscient perspective, begin reviewing your life by going back all the way to the time when you were in your mother's womb. Breathe here, in your mother's womb, as you get the sense of being connected, embraced, and fed only pure love.

See, sense, or feel the energy of the anticipation of your birth, and how the world outside you was being formed in preparation for your birth.

As you breathe deeply, allow yourself to witness your birth, and the arms that greeted you, the mother that birthed you, and the smiling faces in the room.

Take your time to breathe deeply as you re-experience your entrance into this world. If you have an experience or memory of this being a difficult time, then envision how your birth might have happened if the people in your life were awake and were being the enlightened version of themselves. This may be an opportunity for you to "rebirth" yourself and feel or imagine a whole new birth experience with the "awake" version of your family and loved ones.

Take some time in the silence to experience this.

From this wonderful, Godlike, omniscient purview, scan your life as an infant, exploring the world for the first time. Notice the vulnerability, your core-level symbiotic connection with the people around you, nature, music, sounds, your siblings or other beings you relate to on a regular basis.

Now scan your years as a toddler, learning to use language, words, boundaries, emotions. You are coming into a sense of who you are as a unique being. Were you shy? Creative? Outgoing? Explore this important formative time of your life.

Scan your years as a child . . . as a preschooler . . . going to school for the first time, getting used to a whole new form of structure, expectations, and socialization.

Get a sense of the cast of characters in your life: your family, siblings, extended family, neighbors, friends, and community members.

Connect with the feeling tone or energy vibration of your younger years. Get a sense of how the people and events during this time in your life set the tone and shaped the foundation of the way you see the world and interact with it.

See, feel, or imagine yourself entering elementary school. Allow yourself to drop down into memories of significant experiences or mile markers that stand out to you as pivotal moments of joy, trauma, and self-definition.

See, feel, and reexperience how you handled each situation. Pay attention to the moments where you chose the high road and rose to the occasion presented before you.

Notice where you did not choose the high road—where you took the road that wasn't the highest choice. This is not an opportunity to beat yourself up, but simply an opportunity to become aware of how, if given the chance, you would do it differently.

In fact, if there is a particular moment of regret or pain, envision now how you would handle the situation differently, knowing what you know now.

Make sure to review the moments where you did rise to the occasion and did the best you could do under the circumstances you were in.

Now proceed through . . . middle school . . . high school . . . all the way through college age, young adulthood . . . stopping to pause at those critical life-changing moments.

Pause to see what you would have done differently in the moments when you didn't choose the highest route. Pause to reflect upon the moments where you did choose the route aligned with your highest path.

Continue to breathe deeply and feel the inner alchemy as you scroll through your life, advancing further into adulthood, pausing at significant moments that defined and marked your character.

Review your responses. Observe how you behaved when you forgot who you were.

Observe how you behaved when you remembered who you were.

In the moments of forgetfulness, observe how your energy contracted, withdrew, took, and drained the other people around you.

Now see the same situation from the perspective of what you would have done differently if you remembered who you were.

See yourself handling every situation from a place of true remembering.

Now bring yourself all the way to present day, where you are right now in your life.

See the circumstances, challenges, opportunities, and people in your life now.

Where do you fall prey to forgetfulness?

Where do you find it easy to remember who you are, and thus act accordingly?

Envision, feel, or imagine that you are totally awake in your life today, feeling a continuous sense of connectivity to source, love, and enlightenment . . . operating from the overflow of your being.

Notice the way you envision handling the situations and circumstances that most challenge you in your life differently—from a place of being completely awake.

Now go beyond your present life, and project yourself into your future.

See yourself proceeding in your life as an awakened being with a primary reference point in the Remembrance of who you are and remembering the truth of the other beings in your life (fellow lottery winners that forgot they are lottery winners).

Envision moving forward all the way to the moment of your transition from this world into the next. See, feel, or imagine that you are totally awake as you transition from this plane of existence to the next—you are fearless, awake, in full Remembrance of the mighty, spiritual, light-filled, phenomenon that you are.

And now go beyond your death.

See, sense, or feel your body dissolved into pure light, your soul unscathed by the illusion of death.

You are now truly conscious and awake on an even greater, more expanded level than before, glowing, and radiant.

And with these next few breaths, find yourself back in the Life Review Theater, where you began this holographic life review.

With these next few deep breaths, feel yourself integrating all the wisdom and love you've just experienced in this wonderful journey of Remembrance. Feel and sense the healing effect of this holographic life review and how it has altered your perception. Feel and know that you are not the same person that began this journey. You are more yourself—your true self—than ever before.

Carry this awareness with you into your sleep, into your waking reality, and into the rest of your life.

RAS: The Bouncer at the Nightclub of Our Mind

Neuroscientists believe that at any given moment there are approximately two million bits of information available to perceive. However, most human beings are only capable of perceiving no more than nine bits of information at a time. You don't have to be a mathematical genius to realize that there is more going on in this big, beautiful world than we have eyes to see or ears to hear.

What determines those nine bits of information we perceive, you ask? Excellent question. We all have what's called the reticular activating system (RAS). The RAS is composed of neuronal circuits connecting the brain stem to the cortex. At the base of our brain stem, the RAS acts as the bouncer of an exclusive nightclub. It has its list of the select few people that are allowed in, and the rest (regardless of how well dressed and interesting they are) get rejected.

We tend to recycle similar thoughts throughout the day (a.k.a. beliefs that are formed because we've thought them before, had a strong feeling about them, and committed them to long-term memory). Because these thoughts haven't killed us, in some way we associate them with our survival. Old habits die hard because we associate all habits with survival. It is challenging (actually, nearly impossible) to open the mind of RAS, the bouncer.

I bet you picked up this book in order to learn something new that might help you not only survive, but thrive. Yes? Then try this on for size: What if your repetitive thoughts (80 percent of them) are a repeat of what you thought yesterday . . . and the day before . . . and maybe even the year before? What if the "new" bits of information the RAS has been rejecting from your nightclub hold the key to a breakthrough in your life?

So, how do you tell RAS to open the ropes and allow new people into your nightclub, when the list appears to be written in nonerasable ink?

The answer is to wait for RAS to get sleepy. *A remembered dream can change what/who goes on the list.* Once inside, a fresh dream insight, symbol, or image brings with it a whole new cast of characters that, once you mingle with them, can radically improve your life, and at least expand your perspective.

But what if you don't have a high degree of dream recall? Not to fret! My suggestion for those who grasp dream wisps, or for even those who have spotty dream recall, do your best to retrieve just one aspect of your dream that jumps out to you as ill-fitting, odd, or out of place. I've found that sometimes that one odd symbol can be transformative, elevating, healing, and sometimes life-changing. Take the following dream for example.

"Rosemary Is for Remembrance"

Soon after my beloved fourteen-year-old dog, Woofie, passed away (on Valentine's Day 2012), I had the following dream:

> I'm at a party where everyone is whining about something. I don't really want to be there, but I don't have the energy to leave—I'm feeling stuck. Suddenly my phone rings. It's my friend Cynthia Kersey (who, in real life wrote a book called *Unstoppable*—this is an important detail). She tells me to come to San Diego for her party. To entice me to drive the two hours from L.A. to San Diego she tells me I can have my very own 'Hamlet.' This shocks me—I'm not sure what a Hamlet is. Isn't it a village? At the very least I imagine it to be a quaint Germanic-style condo in which to stay the night. This motivates me to leave from the party and begin making tracks to the 'Hamlet.'

I awoke from that dream, wrote it down as I always do, and circled the word *Hamlet* because it seemed so bizarre and stood out from the rest of the dream. Not to mention even in the dream it hooked my attention and had me switch directions from where I was planted. I couldn't figure out what *Hamlet* meant in the context of the dream, so I put it in the "unsolved mysteries" file.

The next day I went to my local nursery to buy a tree to plant for Woofie's memorial ceremony (yes, Woofie wasn't just a *dog* to me . . . she was family).

I told the sales clerk at the nursery what I was looking for (in a way that some would say was TMI—too much information—but I wanted her to help me get the right tree).

It came to me that every time I lose a dog, they take a piece of my heart with them. And every new dog who comes into my life gifts me with a piece of their heart. If I live long enough, all the components of my heart will be dog, and I will become as generous and loving as they are.

UNKNOWN

"Excuse me," said a woman shopping behind me, "I didn't mean to eavesdrop on your conversation . . . but I just lost my dog a month ago and also looked for the right kind of tree or bush to plant in her honor. I planted rosemary because in the play *Hamlet* Ophelia hands Hamlet a sprig and tells him, "Rosemary is for remembrance.""

My jaw dropped to the ground. And then she showed me the locket she wore around her neck, containing a small photo of her golden retriever. Engraved on the outside was an image of a rosemary sprig and the quote "ROSEMARY IS FOR REMEMBRANCE. —HAMLET."

To that the sales clerk said, "We just received the most beautiful rosemary bush; it's right next to you."

It was love at first sight: This gorgeous four-and-a-half-foot rosemary bush with tiny lilac-colored buds went home with me and stands gloriously in honor of Woofie, as well as for the remembrance of how much she meant to me.

Besides leading me to find the perfect bush to plant for Woofie's memorial, this little dream wisp—that was out of character with the rest of my dream—served to elevate my spirits from my own pity party to find my own "unstoppable" desire to be among the living. With this dream synchronicity (one that my RAS would have never willingly allowed into my inner nightclub) connected me to a higher frequency of thought that was medicinal to my melancholy heart.

One thing I know for sure is that with time everything becomes clear, all questions are answered, what's broken is restored, new trails are blazed, hearts are mended, love returns, and you will look over your shoulder, with a tear in your eye, at life's utter perfection.

MIKE DOOLEY (TUT, THE UNIVERSE)

How to Be a Permanent Resident in the State of Remembrance

There are some people who live in a dream world, and there are some who face reality; and then there are those who turn one into the other.

DOUGLAS EVERETT

The state of *Remembrance* is where you are from, it's your hometown, and as Dorothy exclaimed as she transitioned from sleep to awake, from Oz to Kansas, "There's no place like home!"

As a resident of the state of *Remembrance*, I'd bet that you have

- made a greater difference to the planet than you give yourself credit for;
- changed more lives for the better than you realize;
- contributed more to life than you can fathom.

Many of us suffer because we have mistakenly collapsed our circumstances into our identity and thus *forget* we are truly magnificent (regardless of our bank account, love life, where we live, what we drive, or the shape of our bodies). We human beings so easily fall prey to coveting what we are not, and taking for granted what we are.

Remembering who you are as a spiritual being, and remembering the unique way life expresses through your talents, strengths, and gifts, gives you the opportunity to value who you are, from the inside out. This is why Remembrance is another cornerstone to awakening to the life of your dreams. In spite of yourself, you can actually accomplish quite a lot while semiconscious and sleepwalking. However, when you actually wake up and *remember* who you are, you can consciously get to the business of living the life you came here to live. One of the fastest ways to give yourself a wake-up call to shift from for*getting* to for*giving* is to take an inventory of all that is right and good about you.

Decades ago, I was in an acting class and we had the assignment to go to a public place and hand out pieces of paper to twenty people (strangers, acquaintances, and even a few people that knew us well). On the pieces of paper were written over one hundred adjectives (i.e. kind, weak, strong, likeable, menacing, pensive, friendly, intimidating, shy, etc.). The paper instructed people to check off five adjectives from the list that they thought best described the person who handed them the paper. I went into a crowded restaurant in Santa Monica with a few friends to hand out my twenty sheets of paper, and later in the night when I got them back, I shoved them into a folder and ran to the privacy of my beat-up Mustang to look at them.

Under my car's dim overhead light, I peeked at these papers and went into a state of shock. I couldn't believe the positive adjectives people checked off the list to describe me. Somewhere inside I was expecting the absolute worst (i.e. loser, wannabe, scared, insecure, fake, selfish, clumsy, ridiculous, nervous).

Without consciously realizing it, my opinion of myself was bargain-basement low. This may have been due to the fact that I was always projecting how my life should be ten steps ahead of where I actually was. I foolishly thought, "When I get *there* (wherever "there" was) I would be happy, worthy of love, and okay." At the rate I was going, I was never going to get *there,* and thus continuously feel empty, broken, insecure, and inadequate. I exploded into tears over these twenty precious sheets of paper with anonymous check marks next to so many "positive" adjectives (beautiful, kind, loving, bright, friendly, confident, powerful). What a shock! I had *no* idea people saw so many positive things in me. *"Hmm,"* I thought, *"maybe I could try on another pair of glasses and see myself with a bit more kindness and appreciation? It certainly couldn't hurt!"*

For the next year I kept those papers in my glove compartment to remind me of what was good about me . . . until I could start to generate my own Remembrance Inventory myself. I heard someone say, "What you appreciate appreciates." If you appreciate someone or something, it improves. So I thought, why not begin with me?

I am still a dreamer who dreams *big;* I'm always projecting ten steps ahead of where I currently am. However, I remember to remember to acknowledge the beauty and the bounty that is presently in my life at this exact millisecond; bringing a sense of fulfillment from the present into each unfolding moment propels me into the future of my dreams.

Remembrance Inventory

1. Your turn. Take out your Dream Journal (or a sheet of paper) and make a list of your core strengths and qualities that describe the unique being that is you. (Here's a clue: What do people compliment, thank, hire, or acknowledge

you for? Here are some suggestions: Are you thoughtful, kind, funny, fun, deep, present, organized, efficient, risk-taking, eloquent, spiritual, pragmatic, insightful, harmonious, helpful, intuitive, understanding, creative, ambitions, a shoulder to cry on, etc.?)

2. From the highest perspective, identify a word or two from the list you just made that succinctly describes the core essence of who you are.

3. When you are in a state of Remembrance, how do you feel? What thoughts do you think? What are you inspired to do?

4. What is the difference between who you are when you remember your core essence, versus who you become when you forget?

5. Name a few things you've done right in this lifetime (from the grand things, such as saving someone from a fire, to the little things, such as giving a waitress a large tip).

6. What would change in your life if you were a permanent resident of the state of Remembrance?

7. What is one thing you can begin to do today to start the process of remembering who you truly are and moving into the state of Remembrance?

R Is Also for *Respect*

R is for *Remembrance*—and it is also for *Respect*. I'm sure Aretha Franklin would wholeheartedly agree.

Think about it. If someone was hostile toward you, made fun of you, thought you were ridiculous, pointless, or irrelevant, would you feel inspired to reveal the treasures of your heart and soul to them?

I don't think so.

It seems that the unwritten law regarding the revealing of secrets is as follows: If someone is disrespectful toward you, they are forbidden access to your secret garden. However, if someone deeply loves you, innately honors you, and treats you in a respectful manner, you will be hard pressed *not* to reveal yourself to them. Even if you've been carrying a secret around for your entire life, if someone showed up in your life with ears to truly hear you, you would spill the beans—all of them—eagerly and gratefully.

It is this way with dreams. When we respect them, they open up and reveal their deepest secrets to us. And we get to rejoice and revel in the secrets to the universe that we've always wanted . . . and so much more!

Don't Be So Disrespectful!

I was tossing and turning one night, having an incredibly jagged sleep experience. I was anxiously waiting for news about who was going to publish this book.

"Why hadn't I heard from the publisher already? Surely the fact that I hadn't heard anything was because they were going to pass . . . maybe no one would like the book? But I had a feeling they were the right publisher. Maybe I was wrong."

My bed sheets were in knots, pillows strewn every which way, my husband in the fetal position on the far end of the bed, protecting himself from my thrashing.

Suddenly I heard a voice booming through my unconsciousness, ripping a gash through my anxiety. It was too authoritative to be me (or who I ordinarily identify as me). This voice had the command of a paternal military captain. He entered my restless dreamtime, disgusted with my behavior, and gave me the following scolding and wake-up call:

> "DON'T BE SO DISRESPECTFUL . . . OF YOUR SOUL. Don't you know who you are? Have you really forgotten . . . again? After all we've shown you? You mean to tell me you are placing your well-being in the hands of these . . . people . . . these whimsical, fallible, fragile, temperamental humans? You're going to take all that we've shown you, throw it away, and buy into their momentary belief about you? Don't be so disrespectful... of your soul!"

I sat up in bed with a jolt. I felt as if I'd been slapped upside the head—in a good way—truly shaken awake. My petty worries suddenly felt ridiculous, like the result of programming as relevant as the fear of falling off the edge of the world . . . old, outdated, and useless.

I felt suddenly peaceful and grateful, breathing deeply. My mind, which had been a beehive of worry just moments before, felt suddenly as calm as an ocean breeze.

"Thanks for the reminder. I can't believe I forgot."

Since then when I find I'm with a client grappling incessantly over petty issues related to their self-worth, I'll hear that booming voice reverberating through me and I can barely stop myself from booming, *"DON'T BE SO DISRESPECTFUL... OF YOUR SOUL! How dare you speak so poorly of yourself! Don't you know who you are?"*

I don't know if this insight would have hit me as deeply had I not dreamed about it. There is something medicinal about a dream and the sneaky way it can creep through the filter of our RAS into our psychological programming, altering us in ways our conscious thoughts could never dream of doing.

From this perspective it seems most of the time our circumstances don't warrant our worry. Our anxiety and stress—at least 99 percent of it—comes from us forgetting who we are. When we forget who we are we, by definition, are for-*getting* to remember the infinite, unlimited beings of unconditional love, creativity, and bliss we truly are. Perhaps if we remembered more often that we are connected to everything and everyone, beautiful beyond measure, magnificent independent of accomplishments and temporary circumstances, we would give our soul and our dreams—two sides of the same coin—the respect they deserve. I believe this is the key (or at least one of the big ones) to the awakening we seek.

> *The Master acts without doing anything and teaches without saying anything.*
>
> *Things arise and she lets them come; things disappear and she lets them go.*
>
> *She has but doesn't possess, acts but doesn't expect.*
>
> *When her work is done, she forgets it. That is why it lasts forever.*
>
> Lao-tzu, Tao Te Ching
> *(translated by Stephen Mitchell)*

R Is Not for Ridiculous

In dreams fantasy gets even with the shameless imp reason.
Friedrich Hebbell

When Bethany first came to see me, she called her dreams "ridiculous!" It was as if she, in the telling of her dreams, was embarrassed by the unruly nature of her nighttime dream theater.

Everyone in my dreams is chaotic. All the people (sometimes family, friends, or strangers) seem to be running in opposite directions, doing different things, going back and forth, like Chicken Little running around in a panic, serving a roast dinner with gravy to multiple people who were all in different locations . . . I'm trying to keep the gravy warm, but it's no use! I try to get everyone together and I feel powerless. No one listens to me. Every time I awaken from one of these dreams I feel stressed, anxious, and irritated! I want these "ridiculous" dreams to stop!

My first order of business was to suggest that Bethany stop calling her dreams "ridiculous" and stop treating them like a "redheaded stepchild" (no offense to all the beautiful redheads out there. Last night I actually dreamed I was one). I suggested she approach her dreams with reverence and curiosity and call them something a tad more respectful, like "mysterious" or "bizarre." (I myself had hoped to use a more "respectful" word than *strangest* in the title of my book *I Had the Strangest Dream* . . . but I think my editor was right about the fact that *I Had the Most Glorious, Magnificent, Wondrous, Life-Changing, Alchemical, Powerful-beyond-Measure Dream* would pass over most people's heads. Most people do relate to calling their dreams "ridiculous" or at the very least "strange.")

I asked her what in her waking life might be causing her to feel chaotic, stressed, and disorganized. Bethany shared with me that a year ago she quit her medical career in an attempt to explore a career path that was more in line with her soul, as well as her priority of being a great mother to her children. After a year she had made leaps and bounds in terms of exploring her niche to empower people through her new business. However, she still felt torn about launching her new career and it taking time away from her children.

I asked Bethany to envision that her dream was helping her to solve the case of "How Bethany Can Have It All."

I prodded, "Think of any television show, movie, or crime novel. They all have some wild card yet genius character that offers insight about the case in an absurd, even 'ridiculous' manner. This is also true in real life. Your dreams are like that. As a detective, you have to respect your sources . . . even if they derive their information in ways that are mysterious, bizarre, or seemingly ridiculous to your logical mind. Suspend your cynicism and consider the fact that your dreams (and your dreaming mind) are *brilliant*—a million times more so than your rational mind could ever dream of being. Think about the people that laughed at Picasso, Van Gogh, da Vinci, Einstein, and the Wright brothers. When you scoff at your dreams, when you discard them as being ridiculous, you are discounting the most brilliant, genius, valuable aspect of you."

"Whoa . . . I never thought of it that way," she replied. "Okay, I'll be more respectful of my dreams."

"Within each person there are multiple subpersonalities. In fact we could say that every person is like a parade . . . and the goal of dreamwork is to get the entire inner parade marching in the same direction. I believe your dreams are revealing the fact that your parade isn't in unison, with all your aspects attempting to care for their own needs (get their own gravy) without considering the well-being of the whole *you*. You want to feed everyone in your life the gravy (the extras; the good, rich, delicious principles you've been learning) but it won't happen with you chasing everyone around (including yourself!). Your dreams are clever in that once they reveal a problem, they simultaneously reveal its solution. For example, since your dream theme is chaotic and frenzied, as the director of this movie, how would you prefer the scene to unfold?"

"I lead everyone away from the chaos, away from the brown gravy. I want them to have an experience of the magic of the blue ocean. I feel that it will be the transformation they are looking for. Everyone follows me into the water (with bathing suits on and snorkeling gear in tow). Without any fuss or resistance, everyone (including my family) joins me . . . and they swim with me wherever I lead."

"How does this feel?" I ask.

"The opposite of scattered. I feel powerful . . . confident, in sync with myself . . . like I have access to the energy I need to feed myself (all aspects of myself), my new career, and my family."

Bethany's redirected dream gave her the internal imprint she needed to find grace and ease in the development of her new business, while maintaining balance with her family. At the core of what is working for her is a healthy respect for her soul, and thus a new appreciation, and dare I say reverence for her dreams. And I know if you love and respect your dreams, they will reveal their magic to you.

> *Anything will give up its secrets if you love it enough. Not only have I found that when I talk to the little flower or to the little peanut they will give up their secrets, but I have found that when I silently commune with people they give up their secrets also if you love them enough.*
>
> GEORGE WASHINGTON CARVER

Take It from Harvard

If you didn't already have a reverence for dreams, hopefully by now you do. But let's bring it down to earth and hear about the benefits of dream remembrance from scholars at Harvard.

In a Harvard study published in 2010, researchers determined one of the many functions of dreams is to problem solve.[5] And who among us does not have some problem to solve on a daily basis? Okay, maybe you don't call them problems. Maybe you call them challenges, opportunities, or blessings in disguise. In any case, remembered dreams, according to Harvard scholars, can help you to become a better navigator of life's little (or big, as the case may be) obstacle courses.

In this Harvard study, volunteers practiced moving through a difficult three-dimensional maze in their waking state. Because of the difficulty of the maze, all the participants in this study performed poorly.

After working on the maze for a period of time, half the volunteers took a ninety-minute nap, while the other half stayed awake. Upon awakening, the participants who had a chance to sleep were asked to share their dreams. Half of the nappers recalled their dreams (most of which had something to do with a maze), while the other half of the nappers reported not recalling any dreams.

Those who recalled their dreams were then able to complete the maze in half the time as those who did not nap and of those who did not remember their dreams.

The interesting thing is that none of the remembered dreams described a direct strategy for being able to master the maze. One person said he dreamed about seeing people along checkpoints in the maze and remembering a bat cave he had once toured. Another dreamed of searching for something in a maze. Someone else dreamed about the music that played along with the task.

The lesson may be dreams don't necessarily have to make logical sense or be obvious to have a benefit within our waking life activities.

"It might be that sleep is the time when the brain is tuned to find those types of associations you wouldn't notice during waking," says Robert Stickgold, PhD, an assistant professor of psychiatry at the Harvard Medical School. "It's not that the dreams make no sense. They make wacky sense. If you're a student and you want to do better on the test, you might need to dream about it. The question is, 'How do I get myself to dream about it?' The answer is to get excited about it. You tend to dream about the things you are excited about."

The implication of this study reveals that the sheer act of dream recall, even from a daytime catnap, provided the dreaming participants a tremendous advantage in completing the maze as compared to those who didn't maintain a connection with their dream state.

Yes, there are spiritual and metaphysical reasons to remember our dreams that connect us to a larger perspective. But this study also makes the case that the decisions informed by our dreams will brighten and enlighten our ability to masterfully maneuver through our mundane, waking life. All this begs the question, "How does one remember (or catch) their dreams?"

Dream Catching

If you haven't bought a Dream catcher for yourself, I bet that you've gifted one to someone else, or received one as a gift from a friend. Dream catchers originated in the Ojibwe Nation and were popularized during the Pan-Indian movement of the 1960s and 1970s. The Ojibwe word for dream catchers is *asabikeshiinh*, meaning "spider," because it resembles a spider web. According to tradition, a Dream catcher is meant to hang above the bed of a sleeping person and protect them from bad dreams. The good dreams filter through the web, sliding down the feathers, into the mind of the dreamer. Meanwhile, the bad dreams get caught in the net, and dissolve in the light of day.

There are, however, other legends that say the nightmares pass through the holes and out the window, while the good dreams are caught in the web, then slide down the feathers to the dreamer. This is the perspective I prefer. I don't like the idea of anything unpleasant staying stuck, even if it is just until the light of day. I'd rather that it move on with its business as quickly and gracefully as possible.

I also resonate with the notion of "catching" dreams. Like spiders that spin webs to catch their food, our dreams are soul food that could fly right by us if we don't build a proper net with which to catch them. Recalling dreams is like keeping a spider web intact. If you move from horizontal to vertical too quickly, you will break the spider web and your fine thread to the dream world will break.

However if your movements are slow, deliberate, and mindful as you transition from sleep to awake, then the nearly imperceptible spider web will continue to connect you to the dream world.

Incorporate as many of the following suggestions in your early morning awakening routine, and you will be well on your way to remembering more of your dreams and becoming a masterful dream catcher.

How to Be a Dream Catcher

1. Don't Move a Muscle!

As you lie on the bridge between sleep and awake after a night spent journeying through the multidimensions of your dreamscape, as best as you can, remain in the position you were in while dreaming. Your body's position, the particular crumple of your blanket, and the smush of your pillow are part of the container for your dream. If you have to move too much, your dreams will evaporate like smoke from a genie's lamp. To the best of your ability, maintain the position you were sleeping in, or climb back into bed and do your best to re-create your body's sleep position in order to catch your dreams.

2. What Was I Just Dreaming About?

One of the reasons more people *don't* remember their dreams is because the first question on their mind as they begin to awaken in the morning is "What do I have to do today?" This question leads to a thought process that activates your adrenal glands to go to the races . . . and in seconds flat, your dream is *gone, baby, gone!* However, if you can remember to allow the very first question you ask yourself to be "What was I just dreaming?" you will have a shot at catching your dreams.

3. Rewind, Replay, Review

Now that you've been able to catch a dream, before getting out of bed, press the rewind button in your mind and replay your dreams at least three times. Don't assume that just because you've been able to recall your dream once, while lying down in your sleep position, you will recall it once you move your body. Your dreams take place in the part of the brain where our short-term memory is located. Within just five minutes after the end of your last dream, half the content is gone. And after only ten minutes, 90 percent is lost. In order to transfer your dreams from short-term to long-term (or at least medium-term) memory, you have to review it several times in your mind's eye before making the journey from horizontal to vertical.

4. The Snooze Alarm Is Your Friend

In an ideal world, we wouldn't need an alarm to get up—our bodies would complete their sleep cycle and deliver us to our waking state, perfectly refreshed with detailed dream recall. However, if you are like most people, you need your handy-dandy alarm to make sure you don't sleep through your morning board meeting. For most of us who are engrossed in the enchanted and cozy realm of our dreamtime, the blaring siren of the alarm shoots adrenaline through our veins and sends our dreams back to Never Never Land faster than we can say "WTF was I just dreaming about?" The good news is that if you have to wake up to an alarm, you have the miracle of the "snooze" function:

- Set your alarm to thirty minutes before you have to actually wake up. As soon as you press the snooze button, you are headed right back to dreamland—with an awareness to *pay attention* to your dreams.

- If at all possible, choose an alarm with a sound that will wake you up but not scare the living daylights out of you. I suggest Tibetan bells or instrumental music that inspires you.

- Place your alarm clock where it is easy to reach in order to keep movement at a minimum so that during your snooze you can resume your original sleep position in order to "catch" the dream you were just having . . . or catch a new one.

5. Put Pen to Paper (Physically or Virtually)

The critical last step is to "physicalize" your dream: transferring it from the intangible realm of your dreams to the tangible realm of your waking life. The easiest way to do this is to pick up a pen and scribble (as legibly as you can, please) your dream in your journal, with as much detail as possible.

- Some people prefer to record their dream using a voice-recording app on their phone.

- You may be one of those dreamers who prefer to draw a picture of their dream. If this appeals to you, then go for it!

- Others prefer to roll over in bed and whisper their dream to their lover, husband, or wife (or all of the above—no judgment—whatever works for you). The only challenge with that is you need to make sure you don't interrupt the dream recollection of the person with whom you are sharing your dreams. Unless your beloved has already captured their dream in 3-D, they may be in jeopardy of losing their dream as they get wrapped up in yours. So, make sure whomever you share your dream with has "physicalized" their dream before you share yours with them. That's proper dream-sharing etiquette (more about that in Portal 5—*M Is for Mastermind*).

Questions for Contemplation

1. Regarding dream recall, of the ways listed on the previous pages, what way do you find works best for you?

2. Which of the ways listed on the previous pages will you use tonight (or better yet, incorporate into your dream recollection routine)?

3. What is the most recent dream you can recall?

4. Regarding the issue of remembering who you truly are, what are three qualities that best describe the unique being you are?

5. What is your biggest challenge to remembering who you are? What do you see as a possible solution to remaining in a state of remembrance?

6. What do you imagine your life would be like if you and the people in it were "awake" and in a state of Remembrance?

There is an unseen life that dreams us. It knows our true direction and destiny. We can trust ourselves more than we realize and we need have no fear of change.

JOHN O'DONOHUE

Chapter 5

Portal 3—
E Is for *E*mbodiment

I've dreamt in my life dreams that have stayed with me ever after, and changed my ideas; they've gone through and through me, like wine through water, and altered the color of my mind.

EMILY BRONTË, WUTHERING HEIGHTS

Embodiment: One that embodies something (i.e., "the embodiment of all our hopes"); the act of embodying; the state of being embodied. Example: Mother Teresa was often regarded as the embodiment of selfless devotion to others.

Dream Embodiment

How many times in your life have you heard how simple it is to create the life of your dreams (i.e., to strike it rich, lose unwanted pounds, attract your dream lover, build your empire, heal all sickness, and, in short, have it all) . . . and it really isn't? Or, conversely, if you're like most people, you've been fed messages about how impossible it is to change, only to discover it's not as impossible as it might seem.

In my experience it seems that when we truly desire to experience change in our waking lives, we can. One of the essential steps is to "embody the energy" of the desired state of being before it is actually achieved. Einstein said that time (past, present, and future) is happening simultaneously, so one way to "wake up" is to habituate the way we desire to feel in the future once everything we wish to have, to be, and to create is in place. This is simple, but not necessarily easy.

I also believe the deeper intelligence of our nighttime dreams expresses through its feeling tone or emotion. Whether the dream be scary or ecstatic, when we take the dream deeply into our bodies and allow the feeling tone to speak to us, we attune ourselves to a deeper treasure trove of insights than we do when we simply look at our dreams from a safe distance. This insight may be telling us that the energy we are already embodying isn't serving our greatest unfolding, or it may be showing us on a deep level the energy we should allow to engulf us if we want to quantum-leap into our next level of evolution.

Within this portal you will explore dream alchemy, dream reentry, and techniques to assist you in embodying the heightened energy of your dreams. As you do this, you will achieve a quantum-level boost toward awakening to who you really are, as well as more profound access to living the life of your dreams.

Einstein's Dream

As a young boy, Einstein dreamed he was sledding with friends through the Alps. In his dream he was whipping through the snow and ice so fast he passed his friends and continued picking up speed until he was going faster than the speed of light. As he broke through the light barrier, he marveled at the colors and energy patterns he saw and felt. He was exhilarated and more awestruck than he had ever been before.

The feeling and imprint of this dream was what he chased his entire life. His scientific career, including the theory of relativity, according to Einstein, was a meditation on that dream he had as a young boy.

Perhaps we can learn something from the smartest person in our recent history. If dream embodiment and meditation was good enough for Einstein, then it is good enough for me . . . and hopefully it will be for you, too.

Dolphin Celebration Dream

You might be wise to source your dream advice from one who has a healthy appetite for magical nighttime excursions. If you can't tell by now, I'm a dream enthusiast, dream-life coach (and founder of Dream-Life Coach Training) not because I find dreams mildly fascinating and entertaining. *Au contraire.* You've heard the saying "Never trust a skinny chef." Using that analogy loosely, if dreams were food, I would weigh five hundred pounds. Allow me to share with you one of my most delicious dreams, worthy of embodying.

> I'm waist-deep in the ocean . . . it's daybreak . . . I can smell the sweet, tropical air and taste the salt on my tongue. It feels like Hawaii. I hear the water lapping the rocks beside me. I'm walking slowly, deeper into the ocean, toward the horizon. I'm all alone . . . just me and the ocean . . . or so I think.
>
> Suddenly a dolphin about five feet in front of me leaps out of the water in an expression of pure joy. I feel my eyes welling with tears . . . my immediate response to a miracle. I feel I'm being presented with a great gift and that the universe is on my side.
>
> Before I have a chance to breathe the experience in, another dolphin appears and does a flip, this time off to my left. I am overwhelmed with heart-expanding bliss. I barely have time to find my emotional balance before I see several more dolphins in

front of me off to the right in gravity-defying synchronized flips and twists.

Tears are now streaming down my face; my heart has expanded beyond the confines of my body, and I am past the point of no return. Just when I think I can't handle any more, there's more. Another pod straight ahead of me is dancing on the water, while yet another pod is twirling. It seems the entire ocean is one enormous dolphin celebration, with me in the center of it weeping in pure unbridled awe.

Suddenly I feel my body leaning to the left—not diving into the water headfirst the way I normally would, but leaning into it, like a dolphin. I'm under water . . . with my dolphin family seeing clearly under water (in real life I wear contact lenses, so I haven't opened my eyes under water since I was sixteen years old). I am breathing under water . . . I am part of the pod . . . at home with this blissful tribe. Where are we going? I don't know, and I don't care . . . we are swimming together at the speed of light, intuitively unified, as if we were all a part of one harmonious body, one mind, one heart, one activity. This is "flow" at its finest . . . a true synergistic community.

Later in the dream I'm recounting the story to someone, crying as I tell the tale. I feel a deep regret that it's taken me this long to finally know what "flow" really is. This new understanding of "flow" by contrast makes my ordinary way of being seem so robotic, clunky, and dense.

I seek comfort in the thought, "Well, at least I finally know what 'flow' means. What if I hadn't had this experience at all and went my whole life not knowing? I am grateful these dolphins came to imprint on me a true understanding of what it means to be in the flow of life."

I awoke from the dolphin celebration dream feeling I had been to the moon and back . . . disoriented, blurry eyed, and tenderhearted. I gave my contact lenses a good rinse (I wear the kind you can sleep in). Understandably, due to all the tears I had shed during dreamtime, my contacts were salty and cloudy. I rinsed them throughout the day and couldn't get rid of the fogginess. I put in a brand-new pair. The fuzziness continued. Two days later, still seeing blearily, I went to get my eyes examined, fully expecting to be told I will need a more strenuous prescription. After all, isn't that the way of it? Our eyes (and health, for that matter) worsen over time, right?

Not in this case. To my surprise the eye doctor discovered the reason my contacts were so blurry was because, overnight, my eyesight had improved! For nine years I had been wearing a −4 contact lens prescription. Since my dolphin dream, my new prescription is a −3.5! Did this sudden improvement in eyesight have something to do with my time spent with the dolphins? When I went to bed the night before, my contacts were a perfect match for my eyes. But, when I woke up I experienced a drastic change in perception (literally and figuratively).

I feel a tingling sensation as I write this. My head is buzzing with a vibration that feels higher and more magical than anything human I've ever experienced. I know intuitively the more I ponder this dream and *embody* it, the more I will eventually integrate this heightened vibration into the fabric of my being.

This is one of the most exciting aspects of dreamwork/play— the fact that you can be given direct access to a higher realm of energy (higher than what you normally access during your 3-D waking reality). If you simply take time to embody the energy of dreamtime, the *dreamwork* will brighten, enlighten, evolve, and quicken your personal ability to live your dream life.

For me, my dream dolphins are not just relegated to my dreamtime ocean. My conscious waking life benefits directly from their elevated energy. They are guides I now call on in my waking life when I'm feeling constricted, controlling, attached to an outcome, and needing to realign with the qualities of flow. I can't help but feel that as we evolve as a species, we will become more *dolphin-ian* in our ability to communicate intuitively with one another as we flow with the glow of life.

> *You are adaptive beings . . . and you're not finished as a species in your evolution. You are as unevolved now to what you will be 2,000 years from now, or a million years from now—as the relics that you are digging up of the cave man. You are . . . we are all eternally continuing to evolve.*
>
> ABRAHAM/HICKS

The Bull That Couldn't Sing

Jimmy had been feeling extremely fatigued, experiencing chronic abdominal and joint pain, and noticed he'd gained an additional thirty pounds that he wanted to shed. He knew his diet was probably contributing to his waning well-being but didn't see a clear path of change . . . until he had the following dream:

> I'm visiting my friend Ron in his boyhood home in Canada. He's showing me around his animal corral as he tells me about a bull that once chased him. Just as he says that, the bull appears out of nowhere, comes after me, and traps me between its horns, pinning me against the side of the corral. For hours I'm terrified, standing still, trying not to breathe. I finally realize, intuitively, the bull doesn't want to hurt me, but contain me. I begin to hum a song and the bull nudges me . . . I stop . . . then I start to hum again . . . he nudges me again, and I realized the bull appreciates the vibration of the song. I begin singing "Brass in Pocket" by the Pretenders.
>
> I look down and realize the bull has captured not only me but also a goat. As I'm singing, the goat looks up at me with hope in its big brown eyes, praying that the singing will inspire the bull to release us. Finally the bull communicates to me

(telepathically) that the reason he has me pinned is so that I could sing a love song from him to the goat, because he can't sing. He tells me he's been in love with the goat from the moment they first met and would I please tell the goat that he loves her. He realizes it can never work out between them—he's disappointed about that but accepts it. He hopes they can be friends.

With that, my heart explodes with compassion. I can feel the depth of love from the bull to the goat, and I break into a Frank Sinatra song at the top of my lungs: "I believe for every drop of rain that falls, a flower grows I believe that somewhere in the darkest night, a candle glows."

The bull releases the goat and me . . .but we stay near him. A profound love and bonding has just happened . . . and I weep with compassion for all creatures of the world—thanks to that amazing bull that needed me to be his mouthpiece.

Jimmy is a musician and a music producer, with music being his primary language. His gift in this life is to work with music as a bridge to connect hearts. This dream Activated an interesting life change, however. Jimmy, who had always considered himself an "everything-a-tarian" (he would eat whatever he was in the mood to eat, including red meat) became a strict vegan. He truly *embodied* the wisdom of his dream, and because of the depth of connection he felt with the bull and goat he became startlingly aware of the sentience of animals. Jimmy began eating a plant-based diet, and as a result he lost thirty pounds, no longer has abdominal or joint pain, and is healthier now than he has been in twenty years. And that's no bull!

After silence, that which comes nearest to expressing the inexpressible is music.

ALDOUS HUXLEY

Embodying the FEEEEELING and Winning the Lottery

This story takes place entirely in the waking world, however, I can hardly think of a more powerful story to illustrate the importance of *embodiment* to co-create the life of our dreams:

It was June 28, 2009, and Chili—known by many as the "Life is Good" redheaded angel of New York City—was in a funk. What triggered her dark night of the soul? First, it was her third rejection from a bank for a $25,000 loan she had been trying to get to start her business. Right on the heels of that, Michael Jackson (her favorite musician/entertainer of all time) died on June 25, 2009, *her birthday* . . . and she was inconsolable.

She was so upset that she developed a stabbing migraine headache. She drew the curtains, blocking out the glare of Times Square below, and in her Manhattan apartment, with the covers pulled strategically over her head, she sulked.

This story might have continued spiraling downward if not for a road trip she had planned weeks earlier with her friend Terri (born April 24). Because of this randomly planned road trip back to their hometown—eleven hours away in Detroit, Michigan, she woke up in the morning, popped a couple Advils and made four special road trip compilation CDs to celebrate Michael Jackson's life and amazing spirit.

As Terri and Chili drove they sang at the top of their lungs to "I'll Be There," "Man in the Mirror," and "Don't Stop 'til You Get Enough." As you might imagine, with each mile they drove and each song they sang, Chili's headache receded and her spirits lifted.

In between songs, Chili and Terri played a gratitude game, naming at least two or three things for which they were grateful. For example, Chili said, "I'm grateful that you, Michael Jackson, and I are all from Motown; I'm grateful you talked me into going on this road trip." With each mile they journeyed, past the hustle and bustle of NYC to the gentle rolling terrain of the land surrounding the Great Lakes, in spite of herself, Chili was having a great time.

By the time Chili and Terri arrived in Detroit, it was early evening and her "Life is Good" attitude had reemerged, like the sun from behind a cloud. Terri pulled the car in front of a local pharmacy on Woodward Ave and proclaimed, "We are going to buy lottery tickets!"

Terri got out of the car while Chili waited. But, just as he was about open the door to the pharmacy, Chili burst out of the car, "*Wait!* If we're going to do this, we have to act as if we already won!"

She looked deeply into Terri's eyes and implored, "How would you feel if you won? Feel that energy in every cell of your body!"

Within moments they began jumping and shouting, *"Oh my God, I can't believe we won!"* People stopped to stare, horns honked, it was quite a scene. There was some part of her that knew that they had to feel as if they had already won in every cell of their being.

They agreed to use the numbers 2-4-2-5 to represent their birthdays and the day of Michael Jackson's passing in the "Daily 4."

That night, in the warmth of her family's home, Chili found a balance between the low and the high she had experienced that day while she chatted and watched TV with her mother. Suddenly, out of the corner of her eye, Chili saw the graphic come across the screen for the "Daily 4" and she heard the TV announcer say in a low baritone, "The winning numbers are 2-4-2-5."

In slow motion, Chili called her sister to have her confirm the numbers on the Internet.

"It says 2-4-2-5."

"Oh my God! I won!"

Without taking a breath, Chili's sister shouted, "You—just—won—five—thousand—dollars!!"

"I have five tickets…all with the same numbers."

"Oh my *God!!* That means you just won $25,000!!!"

Shaking and screaming, Chili called Terri to tell (yell) him the great news, and that they would, of course, share the winnings fifty-fifty.

"No, Chili, that $25,000 is all yours! I bought five of my own identical tickets, all with 2-4-2-5!"

What I love most about this story isn't just the fact that my friend won the lottery (five times over), but that this demonstrates how the act of fully *embodying* the energy of your desire or dream, then raising it up a few notches, puts you in league with that which you desire to manifest? In case you missed it, here's the Embodiment Formula:

1. Start with a base of simple gratitude to bring your energy into a space of grace (from the Latin root *gratia*, meaning "thanks").

2. Once you have a basic sense of thanksgiving running through your veins, give your inner child permission to use his or her imagination to play "What If" regarding your desires, and feel as if it were already a reality.

3. Take action inspired by your overflowing feeling (more about this in the next Portal, *A* Is for *Activation*): make

an important phone call, ask your boss for a raise, launch your new business, throw yourself a party, or buy a lottery ticket . . . whatever it is that would be your next bold move toward living the life of your dreams.

4. Let go, let it flow, detach from the outcome, and be delighted by what shows up.

He is rich or poor according to what he is, not according to what he has.

HENRY WARD BEECHER

This story also demonstrates the power of friendship, and how when dream buddies are just as invested in each other's dreams as they are in their own, they both prosper, and literally "double their winnings" (more about this in Portal 5, *M* Is for *Mastermind*).

I often use the metaphor that "we are all lottery winners" (which we are), but it's so great when someone actually embodies the energy of being a winner *before* the proof exists. If we were really awake, we would all be this excited to be alive every day. The fact that you were born makes you a lottery winner! The fact that you are *you,* with all the unique, complex, and even bizarre characteristics that combine to make up your one-of-a-kind being is evidence you've won the prize. The sheer fact that you are breathing while you read this is worthy of celebrating. If this doesn't ring true, then perhaps this is your wake-up call to remember the fact that you are indeed a lottery winner. You would not be here, reading this, were it not true!

Embodiment Meditation

I suggest that you do this meditation prior to taking an action that feels like a *big* deal, overwhelming or scary. By embodying the energy you desire, you will be more likely to succeed in your endeavor. To reap the benefits of this meditation, I recommend you access it in any of the following ways:

- Read the following in a meditative way, slowly contemplating each sentence, breathing deeply with each thought, pausing to close your eyes to take in each element that resonates with you.

- Record yourself reading the meditation (slowly, allowing plenty of pauses between the phrases). Play your recording for yourself to enjoy in a relaxed environment with your eyes closed.

- Download the mp3 of this meditation from *www .KellySullivanWalden.com/meditations*

- Create a relaxed atmosphere for yourself where you won't be interrupted.

- Keep a journal and pen nearby to write down your *aha*s.

Close your eyes and take a few deep breaths.
Let go of any cares or concerns.
Allow each breath to elevate you to a higher and higher place of awareness . . . while simultaneously feeling completely rooted and connected to the love and strength of Mother Earth.
Allow your mind to open all the way . . . as if all the doors and windows of your heart and soul were available to the highest possibilities in this universe.

Begin to feel into what it is you are truly wanting. Think about the action you will be taking and what your desired outcome is. Now take it up a notch . . . allow yourself to feel into the energy of the greatest possibility of this situation. Allow your mind to crystallize this scenario or feeling into a specific image that encapsulates the peak experience you want to embody. Or, if you prefer, you can connect with a peak experience from your past or from a nighttime dream, a memory, or feeling of pure enlightenment and love.

Take your time reviewing the scene or moment you'd like to choose from this elevated moment of high vibration.

See, feel, or imagine the details as specifically as you can. What, in this heightened scene, did you see . . . smell . . . touch . . . taste . . . feel? Allow yourself to dive right into the center of this experience.

Now notice the way this experience inspires you to feel. What are the physical nuances of this energy or emotion?

Where in your body do you feel the intensity of this experience? Do you feel it in your heart, solar plexus, hands, stomach, chest? Grant yourself permission to be saturated by this wonderful feeling . . . let it take over . . . permit yourself to become blanketed by this vibration so that your entire body is consumed in this glow.

As you bask in this sensation, allow the energy to intensify, brighten, and heighten within you. Allow this heightened state to have a life of its own within you. Allow it to lead you and take you where it wants you to go.

Notice wave after wave after wave of this experience coloring your mind, brightening your awareness, altering your cells, reorganizing your DNA, reconstituting your relationship with life, rewiring your awareness, and reuniting you with your most blissful, awake, and aware self.

Identify a word that describes this energy, emotion, state of being.

Once you have crystallized this experience into a single word, speak it silently to yourself three times. See the word painted larger than life on the sky of your mind.

And now, imagine this vibration has effectively become part of the fabric of your being. Begin to gain a glimpse of how the embodiment of this vibration will alter the entire course of your life.

Continue to move this energy further out into your future . . . coloring the entirety of your physical existence here on earth.

Looking back from the future, get a sense of the ways your beingness, and thus your life, improved as a result of your integration of this up-leveled feeling.

How has this embodied feeling affected your relationships, your career, your health, your wealth, your spirituality, your overall sense of peace and ease in your most private moments?

Now, give thanks—enormous thanks—for all you have seen, felt, and experienced in the future.

Einstein said the past, present, and future are all happening simultaneously, and one affects the other. Since you were able to embody this heightened state in the present and in the future, you can also color your past with the embodiment of this energy.

Feel this blissful, heightened state coloring all your experiences from the past . . . going all the way back to the beginning of your physical incarnation. Get the sense that you were connected to this energetic frequency all along. Notice how this awareness changes your perceptive of your life experiences. Notice how it casts a different light on each interaction and brings every memory, even the ones that used to be perceived as upsetting, challenging, or traumatic—to a higher place.

Allow this awareness to alter your experience of who you thought you were and how you relate to yourself.

Now as you breathe, gently allow your past and your future to completely merge with this energy . . . and like a prayer, bring them as one into the present . . . into this holy instant . . . and feel the buzz, the synergy, the elation of knowing that it is right here, right now, fully embodied by you. Allow yourself to become grounded, peaceful, spacious, awake, and to comfortably contain this higher frequency. This, after all, is the real, awake version of you.

Give thanks for the dream, memory, or desire that opened this Embodiment experience for you.

Offer gratitude to yourself for taking the time to embody this precious, life-changing energy and emotion.

When you are ready, gently open your eyes. Take some deep breaths to bring yourself back into the beauty, the bounty, and the bliss of this present moment.

Dream Alchemy

A wise person once said, "Keep your friends close and your enemies closer." This is as true in life as it is in dreams. It is human nature to seek to avoid someone or something you consider unpleasant, threatening, or out of your league . . . even if it is an aspect of yourself. However, learning how to shine a light on that which frightens you (while awake or asleep) puts you on the fast track to self-realization and your ultimate fearless awakening.

When Brandy came to see me, she was suffering from the following recurring nightmare:

> My daughter, Vanessa, and I are in the woods looking at a school that she might attend. I look up and see a mother lion and her cub watching Vanessa. I know they want to devour her. They start running toward us and I scream for Vanessa to run away, diverting their attention toward me. The mother lion pounces on me and pins me on my back. Before she devours me I pick up a stick and throw it (as if she were a dog and we were playing fetch). The lion goes for it and chases the stick, while I take the opportunity to run away. I wake up breathless, knowing we were safe for the moment . . . barely.

Logically speaking I could see why this nightmare was so frightening to Brandy, but I couldn't help but secretly be thrilled by the symbolism. I had a hunch that this nightmare held a key to Brandy's confidence.

I shared with her, "From a quantum physics perspective, you are connected to everything and everyone. You can run but you can't hide from your shadow, nor from your light. You can create alchemy by confronting your F.E.A.R.: *f*ace it, *e*mbrace it, *a*ce it, and *r*eplace it. After all, what you resist persists. Even though it seems scary, I'd like you to reenter your dream—and once inside, view it from the perspective of the lion (as a shadow aspect of you) attempting to empower you with a gift."

With eyes closed, I reassured Brandy she was safe as I led her back inside the dream. She *faced* the lion, and immediately broke into tears when she realized it represented her rage at her soon-to-be ex-husband (hell hath no fury like a mother lion scorned!). She had suppressed her anger, fearing it would devour her, which in turn she feared would devour her daughter.

I guided her to ask the lion to impart its gift to her. She immediately began to entrain to (get in sync with) the lion and she began to shake. She began to *embrace* the lion's power. When I asked her how she felt, she smiled through her tears. "I feel powerful . . . happy," she said. "I'm not afraid of my ex-husband . . . not afraid of my anger . . . not afraid of anything right now."

I knew Brandy *aced* the dream when she shared, "I didn't think I could handle this much intensity . . . but I can . . . it's energy that makes me feel . . . confident. I can't believe I ever pushed this away!"

By the end of the session Brandy had demonstrated the power of the F.E.A.R. formula. She had *face*d her fear, *embrace*d it, *ace*d it, and within a few minutes, she had *replace*d a dream that terrified her into a dream that empowered, not devoured, her.

I've found that it is impossible to reenter a dream and create dream alchemy without creating a real-life ripple effect . . . after the worlds are linked. Knowing this, I shouldn't have been surprised when Brandy called me after her custody hearing. She was ecstatic as she shared with me how she walked into the courthouse with her lion by her side. At no point in the meeting did she break down in tears (like she was historically—and hysterically—known for). She felt carried by an invisible strength that made it impossible to feel intimidated by her soon-to-be ex-husband. She walked out of court awarded full custody of her daughter and full custody of her inner lioness.

Why Bad Dreams Happen to Good People

What would chocolate be without bitter cacao and sugar?

What would music be without notes and silences between?

What would a rainbow be without rain and sun?

I see now that there can be no love without loss, no joy without sorrow, *no peaks without valleys.*

AURORA WINTER

Nightmares happen to everyone. Even the best people on the planet have them. In fact, I'm sure Mother Theresa had plenty of them! Here are two thoughts to alter your paradigm about nightmares.

1. Nightmares are your friend.

2. There is no such thing as a bad dream.

Allow me to explain. Albert Einstein said this is the most important question you can ask: "Is this universe friendly?" After decades of research Einstein found the answer to be an unequivocal "Yes." In other words, the entire universe is conspiring on behalf of your greatest good—this would include the obvious blessings and those that come under deep cover (i.e., nightmares).

Think about it: We are not encouraged by our families, schools, governments, or the media to embrace death—no! We are encouraged to "make it" in the land of the living. Yet, according to mystics and shamans (men or women of power and wisdom), if we can't embrace death, the shadow, or at least the *not-so-pretty* aspects of life, then we can't fully live. This is why nightmares are so important to understand—and even to celebrate—in the light of day and in the darkest hours of our sleep.

During the late 1940s, Calvin S. Hall, a researcher at Western Reserve University in Cleveland, Ohio, compiled more than one thousand dreams and analyzed their content. Out of those dreams he found anxiety to be the most common emotion, with negative emotions reported more frequently than positive ones. Most remembered dreams, it would seem, are bad dreams—which, we could say, is a contributing factor as to why most people don't go out of their way to remember their dreams.

Certain nightmares are more common than others. According to Dr. Patricia Garfield, author of *Creative Dreaming,* dreams of being chased are experienced by 80 percent of people, while more than 60 percent dream of falling. Other common nightmares relate to being naked in public or late for a test.

While undoubtedly unpleasant, these nightmares are not necessarily a bad thing, according to Ann Veilleux, a therapist at

Harmónia: Madison Center for Psychotherapy: "A nightmare exposes things that perhaps you haven't expressed in your life—perhaps fears you didn't know you had," Veilleux says. "It's an outlet and also a way of learning about yourself."

Nightmares serve two functions in that they are either helping you *rehearse* for how you might handle a potential worst-case scenario, or they are assisting you to *vent* out limited beliefs, dysfunctional patterns, or traumas lodged in your psyche (like a bloodsucking tick living rent-free in your body). It never hurts to look at a nightmare from both perspectives so you can evaluate which is most relevant to you.

Rehearsal Dreams

Your subconscious mind's job is to keep you alive and assist you in becoming the best-adapted survivor you can possibly be. In this way, think of your nightmares as an overly vigilant/protective parent whose job it is to constantly get you to remember to wear a sweater, check your tires, double-lock the doors, do a background check on the new guy you're dating, and sniff out potential danger . . . even if none actually exists.

To understand what your rehearsal dreams are trying to help you with, ask yourself the following questions:

- Could this dream be warning me about something or someone in my life today?

- Is there something I need to prepare for (an event, presentation, conversation, confrontation)?

- What preventative action should I take to leverage myself advantageously (write note cards prior to a speech, research information about the company I am planning to do business with, have a preemptive conversation with my spouse)?

- Is there something I forgot to do, say, or create that I can tend to retroactively (i.e., make an amends, send a follow-up email, double-check the bank statement)?

Adora's Rehearsal Dream

Here's an example of a dream/nightmare that gave the dreamer a preview of coming attractions so that she could make a (potentially) life-or-death course correction:

> I'm walking down an alley and I see a red-haired man lumbering toward me. I think I should cross the street to avoid him. I think to myself, "He's socially off." But I feel sorry for him. I don't want to hurt his feelings, so I continue walking toward him. When our paths cross I smile at him and he grabs me, punches me in the stomach, and kicks me repeatedly. I try to scream but I can't. I realize too late I should have listened to my instinct and crossed the street . . . but my disease to please overrode my instincts.

Adora interprets her dream as follows: "The following day I went to a pool party at my friend Maria's condominium complex. I was having a great time and, as always, being the social butterfly that I am in these kinds of situations. Out of the corner of my eye, I notice a red-haired man on the opposite end of the pool—all by himself. I noticed I immediately felt sorry for him. Out of obligation, I found myself swimming toward him to introduce myself. As I neared him, my blood turned cold and memories of being attacked in my dream came flooding back to me. In an instant I switched gears. Instead of chatting him up, as per my M.O., I swam about-face, got out of the pool, and went inside.

"Once inside, I shared my dream with my friend Maria, and she recognized the man as a neighbor who had always given her the creeps. Maria knew his name and looked him up on the Internet and discovered he was on the sex offender registry.

"Even though it was an unpleasant dream, I was grateful for it because it may have prevented me from harm."

Adora remains a social butterfly yet maintains an increasing respect for her dreams that continue to assist her in discerning when to chat someone up and when to cross the street (or swim away).

Venting Dreams

From the perspective of a *venting* dream, consider your subconscious mind's other job (besides keeping you alive, as in the work of rehearsal dreams) is to assist you to thrive. Think "out with the old, in with the new."

If you really want to do an extreme makeover on your life, you need to get out the wrecking ball and start from scratch. Your venting dreams are providing you with a blank slate from which to begin your new and improved dream-life. Your venting dreams are helping you release what no longer serves you while simultaneously helping you call in that which does.

Here's a list of the usual suspects, the common themes that tend to be the fodder of our valuable but less-than-pleasant venting dreams.

1. Death/Dying

Contrary to popular belief, dreams of death or disaster are not a bad thing! Your dreams may be giving you an edge on how to best survive and thrive in your current life circumstances. These dreams may also be helping you to gain a paradigm shift about the things you fear most that keep you from fully living. Often a dream of death or destruction represents that you are at the end of a chapter in your life, just as the next chapter is simultaneously being written. Dreaming of someone dying—or making their transition—is about transformation and change in your relationship. May this dream inspire you to ponder an aspect of your life that may be coming to a close, and how you can more harmoniously participate in the transition. Voltaire said, "It is no more surprising to be born twice than once; everything in nature is resurrection."

Embody the feeling tone of release, as well as the energy of the new aspect of life that is emerging.

2. Falling

Dreams of falling signify feelings of loss of control, insecurity, overwhelm, or lack of confidence. You may be losing your step as a result of not having your feet firmly planted on the earth. Or you may be in a growth spurt in your life, experiencing changes, and thus feeling that you're in over your head. You may be judging yourself for having failed at something you set out to do. It is also believed there are "falling spirits" that are beckoning you to them so they can initiate you into a deeper level of wisdom, power, and awareness.

Embody the feeling tone of groundedness to the bedrock of the here and now.

3. Chasing or Being Chased

Dreams of chasing or of being chased signify that you believe what you need is out of reach. You have forgotten that you are the hunter and the hunted. In other words, we are either hunting our power or being hunted by it. Awaken from the seductive thrill of the hunt. Stand still and allow the disowned aspect(s) of yourself, like puzzle pieces, to magnetically integrate and click into place. Let them find their home within you.

Embody the feeling tone of your power.

4. Zombies, Monsters, and Ghouls . . . Oh My!

Dreams of a zombie represent a part of you or someone in your life that is sleepwalking, being mindlessly controlled by someone or something beyond one's own internal GPS. Dreams of monsters and ghouls (a.k.a. shadow creatures) symbolize your dark side (hey, don't shoot the messenger: Every character in our dreams represents an aspect of us, the beauty and the beast, the fertilizer and the flower). Ghouls and monsters represent that which is unintegrated, rejected, or perceived as unacceptable and thus suppressed. Keep in mind that it is only a shadow creature until you've embraced it in the light of your awareness.

Embody the gift of your shadow into the light of your being.

5. Graveyard/Cemetery/Tombstone

Dreams of a cemetery/graveyard/tombstone represent a distinct change or the ending of a cycle, such as a relationship, business affair, or significant Portal in your life. You may be grieving and moving through the bittersweet sorrow of missing your connection to a loved one or you may be releasing a cherished attachment. Keep in mind the motto, "Keep what you want, and leave the rest behind."

Embody the feeling of relief because you no longer need to carry unsupportive energy from the past.

6. Witch/Old Woman

Although scary, an old witchy woman (a.k.a. crone) in a dream symbolizes great wisdom and empowerment. Sometimes a witch or an old woman represents darkness, jealousy, or vindictiveness. A metaphysical interpretation of the crone, however, is that she is a primary instigator of spiritual growth that ushers someone who is stuck in unconsciousness to find their conscious power. Because the crone doesn't have a people-pleasing bone in her decrepit old body, she represents independence, freedom, and authenticity and one who makes up her own rules.

Embody your irreverent power and ability to create magic in your life.

7. Blood

Dreams of blood symbolize life force, power, and connection to your family or spiritual source. If you are bleeding in a dream, consider that there may be a place in your life (or a relationship) where your power is leaking.

Embody the strength of your ancestral lineage.

8. Skeletons

Dreams of a skeleton can reflect the foundational structure of your business, relationships, or your belief systems in general. If the bones in the skeleton are strong and healthy, then so is your foundation. If the bones are weak or brittle, then it is time for you to strengthen your foundation from the inside out. Also, skeletons can represent secrets that are scratching at the closet door to be revealed.

Embody the power of transparency; having no secrets and nothing to hide or be ashamed of.

9. Mask

Dreams of a mask can represent shame about your authentic self; fear that you are not good enough, powerful enough, or strong enough; and an unwillingness to reveal the real you. Keep in mind that sometimes the wearing of a mask is a necessary step of evolution until your ego has integrated the power the mask symbolizes, at which point, the mask is no longer necessary. Masks also represent ancient symbols of power, evoking the medicine (qualities) of the gods or goddesses they represent.

Embody the energy of authenticity.

10. Departed Loved Ones

When you dream about someone you love who has crossed over, you might feel that you've actually had a visit with them . . . because maybe you have. Pay particular attention to the dream situation they come cloaked in and to the words they convey. These dreams are often literal, requiring a minimum of interpretation and a maximum of meditation. At the very least you can feel grateful for having a connection not only with your departed loved one, but also with life beyond your five senses and all that resides on the other side of the veil.

Embody love, strength, and guidance from your departed loved one(s).

The next time you lift your head from your tear-drenched pillow, awakened from a scary dream, give thanks for these dreams that are instigators of transformation, wisdom, and enlightenment, if you allow them.

Dream Reentry

Carrie came to see me to discuss the following dream:

> In my dream I see an overweight young woman wearing a thick fake mustache, a hat and glasses (à la Bonnie & Clyde) sitting in the backseat of an old jalopy, eating crunchy candy (like a lollipop). I walk up to her to get a closer look but she is so fixated on eating her candy, she is oblivious to me getting near her . . . she is like a zombie.

Even though this might not seem like the scariest of dreams (no blood, knives, or chasing) Carrie was deeply disturbed by this image upon awakening. When she came to see me I taught her *Dream Reentry*, a process by which you

1. re-envision your dream in the waking state;

2. imagine redirecting your dream to unfold in a way you would have preferred;

3. repeat several times until the nightmare literally becomes a sweet dream.

I asked Carrie, "Imagine you are the director of the movie. From this perspective, what would you prefer would have happened? You can either pick up the dream where it left off or change it entirely."

Carrie quickly replied, "First I would take off that fat suit! Under the fat suit would be a lean, lithe version of . . . me. (Carrie had been struggling with weight issues—layers of numbness covering her bright spirit.) Next I would drop the disguise (the mustache and hat) that hides my real, autonomous, creative, wild, funny, sexy aliveness. I would drop the candy, because I know it isn't good for me and the only thing it's helping me to do is numb out. Then I would get out of the backseat of that old jalopy. I would have a brand-new, convertible sports car, and I would hop into the driver's seat (power position) and take off, away from that place toward someplace new and exciting!"

When I asked Carrie how her newly imagined dream left her feeling, Carrie replied with tears and a smile: "Fantastic, free . . . me!"

It seems that every time I go looking for something small, the Universe hands me something bigger and better. What if I could trust that and relax into it? What if everything is working out exactly as it is supposed to?

AURORA WINTER

I believe that nightmares are unfinished dreams: every dream is a gift and a blessing. Even the scariest, most unpleasant, and gory dreams come bearing gifts—if you have the eyes to see them.

Normally when I am on a radio show I'm asked typical questions like "Why are dreams so difficult to remember?" "What does it mean if your teeth are falling out?" "Why are dreams so hard to understand?" I always enjoy hosting and being a guest on radio programs, but, I must admit, after answering the same questions five million times over the last few years, it can get a bit, shall we say, routine, like driving home the same way from work. However, on June 8, 2011, I was thrown for a loop on one of the most memorable shows to date for me. I was the guest on a web radio show called *The Attitude Shift* with Donna M. Butler and Siobhan Shaw . . . and boy, did it shift my attitude toward live radio! Here's what happened.

I was debunking the "Three Dream Myths":

1. Some people don't dream (everyone dreams between three and nine dreams every night).

2. Dreams don't matter (I list inventions and contributions to science, medicine, arts, and entertainment that were birthed into this dimension via dreams).

3. There is such a thing as a "bad dream."

After addressing the last myth I quickly added, "This doesn't mean we don't have unpleasant, scary, or traumatic dreams . . . however, when we learn how to work with them, we reap the medicine within them and see how they can propel us forward on our life path in a truly positive way."

To that, Donna, the show's co-host, challenged, "Well, I've had a recurring nightmare for the past twenty-five years that has been truly debilitating; it's cost me relationships and homes and has been keeping me up at night for two and a half decades. I'd love you to show me how this isn't a 'bad' dream."

I asked her if she would be willing to share her dream, and she did:

For the past twenty-five years I have a nightmare once a week where I walk through my living room and as I get in front of the window that faces the street I hear myself saying, "This is where I get shot." At that moment, the glass is shattered with a gunshot and a bullet penetrates my chest and I wake up gasping.

"At first I thought if I moved to a new house the dreams would stop," she said, "but they didn't. Because of this dream I've moved a dozen times, and regardless of where I live, I have the same dream. It always takes place in the living room of the house I happen to be living in. This nightmare haunts my waking life and causes me to be nervous and cautious, not to mention causing me to avoid my living room. When guests come over they all know that we never sit in the living room, only in either the kitchen or my bedroom. If I have to get through the living room I will run . . . and when I do, I hear myself say silently and sometimes out loud, 'This is where I get shot.' On some level, I expect that this is how I will die—by getting shot in my living room in real life."

I asked Donna about the reality check aspect: "Do you live in a place where this is likely to happen, or has this type of thing happened to one of your neighbors? Did this happen to you when you were growing up? Did you ever know of this happening to anyone you've known?" To all the questions Donna's answer was no. There didn't seem to be a rational explanation for this strange recurring nightmare.

I told Donna I see recurring dreams as cosmic highlighter pens instructing you to "drill here." In my experience, a nightmare is an unfinished dream. Once you receive its gift, then it is complete, and you can use your dreamtime for new (and hopefully more pleasant) insights and experiences.

"Would you be willing to tap into your *imagic*nation to reenter the dream in order to redirect it, find its gift, or at the very least, complete it?" I asked her.

Teary, she said yes.

I asked her to let me know when she had reconnected to the dream.

In a shaky voice she said, "I'm here."

I asked her to explore who it is that is trying to shoot her.

At first she said, "I don't know. It's dark outside." When within a few moments she gasps, "It's my father!," she then tells me, "My father is mentally ill (Alzheimer's and dementia) and I haven't seen him in twenty-five years." (This was about the amount of time she'd been having this recurring dream.)

I asked her to bring someone into the dreamscape to give her strength and protection to help her confront her father. She chose her best friend and co-host, Siobhan Shaw.

In Donna's reentered dream, the two women walked out in front of the house together to approach Donna's father.

Donna began to cry. "He is showing me the peace sign."

I instructed her, "By using your breath, give back to your father the fear he gave to you. Take back your power that you gave to him. Get rid of what isn't yours, and reclaim what is yours . . . let your power and your peace come back into your body."

She spent several minutes breathing in this way, crying, and eventually let me know that she felt that she had given him back the fear she got from him and taken back the power and peace she gave to him.

Donna told me she felt her energy shifting and that she was no longer afraid of him. He's now just a scared, little old man who wanted to get her attention. She gave him the peace sign and took off her dark glasses. (Donna is famous for always wearing her dark glasses . . . even at night.)

She gasped and told me that he was showing her a favorite childhood memory: flying kites. "We used to have so much fun together . . . laughing and playing. I can even smell his Old Spice . . . I forgot about his Old Spice . . . I forgot about the kites." Donna went on to say, "All these years the only thought I've had about my dad is how afraid of him I've been and what a basket case he's become. I forgot about who he *really* is. I forgot he really did and still does love me."

She gave her dad a hug and watched him get into his car and drive off. She walked back into her house and stood in front of her living room window, in peace.

I congratulated her for her courage and began to interpret her dream's symbols:

A *window,* as opposed to a wall, can be seen as a place of vulnerability, a place, like our hearts, that can be shattered. But, just like a broken window, a broken heart can be mended—with love and attention. And, once the heart is healed, the wisdom radiated through the window of the heart is exponential.

Death or dying in a dream, especially in a shocking and abrupt manner, suggests to me that there is a pattern wanting to die so that a new one may emerge. Being shot in a dream is usually a message to end a pattern in an abrupt way.

Six months later I was invited back to *The Attitude Shift* and Donna happily shared with me that she now *loves* sitting in her family room in front of a plate-glass window with the drapes wide open. In fact, she just fulfilled one of her lifelong dreams and opened a bakery where she makes the best king cakes and cupcakes in St. Francisville, Louisiana, while looking out a big, beautiful shop window.

Donna said, "Prior to our radio show/dream healing session, I never would have opened a business that is so exposed via a plate glass window to the world walking by. Not only do I feel unblocked, but also the terror I carried for twenty-five years was lifted off of me with one dream session. Because I took advantage of the 'window of opportunity' my recurring dream offered me, I feel at peace regarding my dad, and I am no longer afraid of plate-glass windows and all that they represent."

Along these lines, the following dream story represents the tremendous life-transforming ability our dreams have to be agents of change and alchemy in our lives . . . if we work them.

I met Dara when I was a speaker at Aurora Winter's Grief Coach Academy. During my presentations I often call on a volunteer to demonstrate the power of dream alchemy and its ability to turn water into wine, drama into phenomena, and the tragic into magic.

I asked the audience if anyone had an unpleasant dream they would like to work on with me in front of the group. I saw Dara's shaky hand rise in the back of the room. I felt chills move up my spine as I called on her. She looked shocked. She couldn't believe I would pick her when there were so many other willing volunteers that were more demonstrative than her.

She tiptoed up to the front apologetically. Clearly she was not used to being in front of large groups, much less talking about something deep and intensely personal. But she summoned the courage and shared with me her recurring nightmare. (A word of caution here: This story has a happy ending, but it is a gory path to the glory in this case.)

> I rarely dream . . . I try not to dream . . . because when I do it is horrific. The last time I saw my husband was at the scene of the car accident where he died. His body was in pieces scattered across the road. It was worse than my worst nightmare realized. When I dream I am haunted by this horrible scene . . . in fact, in my dreams it is worse . . . bloodier and gorier. I wake up wishing I were dead. I am grateful for the days when I wake up dreamless. I just pray that the images will stop haunting me.

You could have heard a pin drop in the room. The only sound was Dara's tears. I thanked her for being so courageous to share her dreams and her story. I acknowledged her for being brave to have survived such an experience, and for showing up at the Grief Coach Academy for help that would eventually help others.

I told her, "On the level of the dream, shamans from indigenous tribes (Australian Aborigines, Senoi from Malaysia, Iroquois from North America, etc.) believe that a nightmare is an unfinished dream. In the case of the Senoi, they were trained to go back to sleep to "complete their dream" so that it would end in a way that gave the dreamer back their power. These shamans also believe there is a relationship between the nighttime dreams and our daytime reality, and if you complete a nighttime dream, you will experience some form of completion, clarity, or wisdom in your waking life. Are you willing to go back inside your dream with the intent of completing the dream?"

Dara nodded her head.

I asked her to close her eyes, take some deep breaths, and to surround herself with a brilliant bright light. To allow herself to feel completely loved, protected, and safe, I told her this light would be with her as she reentered her dream. I asked her, when she felt sufficiently connected to this light, to nod her head indicating she was ready to reenter her dream. After some time, Dara took a deep breath and nodded her head.

I asked her to describe to me what she saw, felt, and/or experienced.

Dara restated her nightmare: "The dream is a lot like the real-life scene of the accident, just a bit more exaggerated. There are sirens everywhere, ambulances, police, and demolished cars with pieces of smashed metal strewn all over the place. There is blood, and bloody flesh all over . . . pieces of my husband scattered all over the street."

"Thank you. Now, Dara, if you were the director of this dream, which you are, how might you change things?"

"First of all, he never would have been at this intersection in the first place; he wouldn't have been in his car."

"How does that feel?" I asked.

"Unrealistic. He drove to work that way every day."

"Okay, so within the integrity of the dream, how might you change it, or finish the dream?"

She said, "I would be there in the scene, and I would sense my husband's (Tom's) spirit that survived the crash. He would be like an angel in a spirit body. He would pick up the pieces of his body, and like the bionic man, rebuild himself."

"Okay, watch how he picks himself up, and puts his pieces back together again."

"He's back together now," said Dara, beginning to smile.

I said, "One thing I've noticed over all the years I've been doing dreamwork is that when something or someone is broken, then reunited or put back together again, they don't come back in the exact same way they once were—there is something additional about them, an extra layer of wisdom, strength, or ability that in some way justifies the break and makes it worth it. In Spanish they use the term *vale la pena,* which translates to "it's worth the pain." See if you can detect what is extra, better, wiser, stronger about your husband now that he is put back together."

Dara began to smile, to glow. "Tom is just as handsome as ever, but he is more muscular, like when he was younger; it's like he has supernatural strength . . . and he has his hair back! Wow, he looks amazing!"

"Now that he is put back together, what does he do?" I asked.

"He picks me up. He is so strong he lifts me up and takes me flying with him. He shows me heaven . . . he shows me this beautiful place he has been exploring for the past year. It is amazing. Wow, I had no idea. He tells me that he will be here for me when it is my time to cross over . . . but it's not yet . . . not for a while. I still have a lot to do while on earth.

"I don't want him to bring me back to earth. He tells me I can call on him in my dreams to show me around the afterlife. I don't need to stay stuck on the images of his death. That was just one moment in time. There is a lot of beauty that has happened before and since then that I can attune to, if I'm open to it. *Yes!* I'm open! I didn't know!!

"He brings me back down to earth, to my bed, kisses me, and tells me he loves me and that he is here for me . . . in some ways, better than before. I really like that he has his hair back. So does he!"

"Great work, Dara," I said. "Now rewind your redirected dream back to its highest peak. What was your favorite moment in this new dream?"

"When he was holding me in his big, strong arms, flying with me through heaven," she answered. "I could feel his love and strength. I knew he was back together . . . only better than before."

"Great job. Now take a snapshot of that moment and emblazon it in your mind, etch it deeply, by exaggerating the colors, the feeling tone, the smell . . . make it bigger than life, let this wonderful feeling completely overwhelm you and deeply embed itself in your subconscious mind, like a tattoo that cannot be erased, this new image of Tom holding you and carrying you is becoming stronger and stronger, meanwhile the other image is beginning to fade and recess, like impermanent ink that fades and softens over time, until it becomes barely perceptible."

Dara nodded in agreement.

I went on: "The image of Tom holding and carrying you is becoming a dominant thought, around which your feelings, thoughts, and even life view are becoming organized and recalibrated."

Dara was crying, nodding her head, smiling.

The next day, I barely recognized this smiling woman when she shouted at me from across the room: "Kelly, I had a dream last night . . . a real dream! I dreamed I was in the grocery store, shopping, and I had a full cart of fresh groceries! What does that mean?"

I told her, "Symbolically speaking, shopping represents choice to me. When someone is shopping in a dream, to me it represents that they have options regarding the many ways they can "feed," nurture, or nourish themselves . . . that they are "shopping" around for options about what may be best for them. If it was my dream, I would feel that I have choice in my life and that I can now start feeding myself the love/nourishment my soul has been starving for. It's not that the love and nourishment hasn't been here all along . . . but perhaps you didn't know how to receive it (or shop for it and how to load your grocery basket with it)! Perhaps you now feel you can 'feed' yourself in an abundant, healthful way. The images and thoughts you had been feeding yourself over the past year had made you weak. Now you are freed up to nourish your soul in a way that could truly strengthen your spirit, heart, and body. Bravo!"

Months later I was again visiting the Grief Coach Academy. Everyone in the room asked me, "Have you seen Dara? She is a different person!"

When I finally saw Dara, she was seated in the front row of the event (not in the back row like before). With her erect posture and beaming, beautiful smile, she looked ten years younger. She hugged me so tightly I thought my ribs would break.

She said to me, "I carry the image of Tom carrying me around with me wherever I go. I think about it every day, and I literally feel like I am in this stream of not only his love, but also higher love that is bigger than I've ever known. I also feel hopeful that I will make an excellent grief coach because of what I now have to offer. If someone like me could go from heartbreak to happiness . . . anyone can!"

Dream Theater

When I was doing research for my book *I Had the Strangest Dream . . .: The Dreamer's Dictionary for the 21st Century*, I came across Robert Moss's startling data about the ways the Iroquois indians conducted a social form of dream therapy. The Iroquois, dating back to 1100 AD, regarded dreams as the secret wishes of the soul and that it was the duty of a caring community to gather around a dreamer, help him or her recognize the soul's wishes, and take action to honor them. Thus became their social form of dream therapy. Members of the tribe would act out their dreams and were allowed to go beyond the usual disciplined and moral social boundaries. This included making love to another person's spouse. Such hidden desires were seen as the basis of social as well as individual problems. Allowing the expression of unconscious desires was the Iroquois way of conquering sickness of body and mind.

Upon reading about this I became inspired to create my own version of Dream Theater—a space for people to express their dreams in a theatrical way to help them fulfill the intention of their dreams.

As I mentioned, one way of looking at a nightmare is as an unfinished dream. And more often than not, we are awakened before the dream is able to complete its intention, and thus we are left with a constant cliffhanger. I believe that the goal of our dreams is to ultimately remind us that we are whole, perfect, and complete, and that all the running around all day to prove how worthy we are is ridiculous.

What would happen if we could actually extend our dreams to their natural conclusion? If we did this often enough, perhaps we would run out of things to be afraid of and instead realize we are victorious, magnificent beings truly capable of co-creating a heavenly world. In Dream Theater, dreams are brought to life. By seeing dreams acted out with fellow dreamers, we learn to decode the message of our dreams, and most importantly, *redirect* them to unfold in a way that reconnects us with our power, freedom, and peace.

Dream Theater, Jenny & the Rope

The best way out is always through.

ROBERT FROST

In a Dream Theater group session, one member, Jenny, shared the following dream with us:

> I'm surrounded by a council of elders whom I deeply admire. They are teaching me how to make a rope. They tell me to take my rope into the next room for an important mission. They tell me to find something sturdy in the room to tie one end of the rope to. I was to tie the other end of the rope around the neck of a girl who would be in the room and throw her out an open hole in the floor. I was disturbed and confused by these instructions. Did they want me to kill her? I assumed they must know more than I, so I gathered the rope and entered the room. It was like a hotel room: two beds, a dresser, and a big hole in the floor, with a young teenage girl sitting across the room on the far bed. Filled with anxiety, I tried to focus on my task. I tied one end of the rope to the dresser and made sure it was secure. Then I turned to her and asked if she knew what I had to do. She nodded.
>
> "Do you want to die?"
>
> "No. But they want me dead, so just do what you have to do."
>
> I thought, "I can't kill her if she wants to live. There must be another way!" So for hours I talked her into being better-behaved. I told her that I would tell the elders that she had grown up and that we didn't need to kill her. All could be well and no one would have to die. She agreed and thanked me. I held her while she slept.
>
> The next morning I readied myself to go tell the elders that the girl wanted to live. I opened the door and was met by an

angry mob. The elders were furious when they saw the girl still alive. They gathered around me yelling at me to kill her. I tried to reason with them but no one would hear me.

Suddenly the girl came out of the room and screamed, "Stop it!" in the most screeching voice I had ever heard. "I hate you all!" she screamed. "Just get it over with and kill me!!"

I was horrified; I did not want to be a part of this. So I got down on my hands and knees, pushed my way through the crowd, and ran. Then, thankfully, I woke up.

I thanked Jenny for the courage to share her dream with the group. I reminded her, "A nightmare is an unfinished dream. You are the director of your dream theater and you have a say in the matter of how this dream turns out. With that in mind, how would you like to redirect this dream, or pick it up where it left off (within the integrity of the dream)?"

Jenny shared the following scenario, which the group reenacted with her: "The first thing I would want to change would be to have the elders give me back my free will and remove any *have to*s from their communication. They would show me how to make the rope and tell me I had been selected for a very important mission. They would honor me for agreeing to participate. They would go into the room *with* me and help me make the decision about the girl—but they would agree that ultimately they would honor any decision I made."

The group reenacted this scene with her; the "elders" went into the room; Jenny anchored one end of the rope to the woman playing the part of her soul (in my Dream Theater workshops, someone always plays the role of the dreamer's soul). With the other end of the rope, Jenny approached the girl:

"Do you know what I have to do?" Jenny asked.

"You have to kill me," answered the girl.

"I don't think I do actually. I'm just supposed to give you the rope and encourage you to jump out that hole in the floor."

"I don't want to die. I'm scared."

Jenny turned to the elders and asked them for guidance.

They replied, "Sometimes it takes a leap of faith to get to the next stage in life. It might not be death in the way you think. It might just be an even greater experience of *life.*"

Jenny and the girl resonated with this point of view.

"I'm still scared," the girl said.

"So am I," Jenny said. "I will go with you. You and I are connected to our soul . . . and we have our family of elders if we need any assistance. It will definitely be an adventure, but we won't be alone."

Together, Jenny, the soul, and the girl held onto the rope, sat at the edge of the hole, counted to three, and *jumped!*

> *What the caterpillar calls the end of the world, the master calls a butterfly.*
>
> RICHARD BACH

After Jenny's redirected Dream Theater experience, she expressed the following: "I feel like alchemy has just taken place within me. I walked into the dream group riddled with anxiety from the dream and the way I was interpreting it. Because of the dream I can see I have been working through my angst around my family drama. They deeply disapprove of my creative, alternative lifestyle. I've felt outnumbered and overwhelmed by them, and our arguments feel annihilating. My original dream felt debilitating, harsh, and like there was no room for me in my own life . . . and my only choice was to *run.* By the end of the Dream Theater I felt integrated. Instead of hanging myself by my own rope, I threw myself a rope (a lifeline of my own making) and jumped into a (w)hole new aspect of my life. I, strangely, feel 'whole,' like my wise inner committee members are all on the same page so I don't have to feel divided against myself. I feel rewired into *knowing* I am connected to my soul and to the soul (even if I'm not connected to the ego/personality aspect) of my family."

Name It, Claim It, and Reframe It

Here's an encapsulation of how to redirect your dream within a Dream Theater in the privacy of your very own bedroom (for a more detailed, step-by-step explanation for how to create Dream Theater, see Portal 5—*M* Is for *Mastermind*).

Name It

You can't heal what you can't feel. In order to create dream alchemy, you must first go back to the scene of the crime. This works on your nighttime dreams as well as your waking dreams. As painful as it may be, naming the issue is half the battle. Summon your courage and name the issue your dream is revealing (i.e., issues regarding money, power struggles, job security, weight/body issues, health, healing, rejection, etc.). Now identify how you feel as a result of this scene (i.e., frightened, disrespected, restricted, abandoned, powerless, rejected, disliked, dishonored, etc.).

> *We cannot change anything unless we accept it. Condemnation does not liberate, it oppresses.*
>
> CARL JUNG

Claim It

Once you've named the primary issue and core feeling(s) this dream situation brings up for you, take some deep breaths, and simply be with this uncomfortable feeling. This may seem counterinstinctual, but breathe anyway, and while you are breathing, make room inside yourself for this discomfort to exist. We are trained to pull back from the fire, to run from pain, and to recoil from ugliness, which is an appropriate response during an early period of our development but counterproductive if we choose to transform into a more awakened version of ourselves. In order to create mastery over it, the name of the game is to *open wide* and embrace it all.

As you breathe, imagine the interior of your consciousness as a vast ballroom, with room for all aspects of you to get a spotlight dance. The classic fairy tale "Beauty and the Beast" demonstrates this principal to a tee. In the story a lovely maiden (Belle, French for "beauty") falls in love with a hideous beast (a.k.a. the unintegrated shadow) and in so doing breaks the curse and transforms the beast into a handsome prince.

Reframe It

Poison leaves clues. Isn't it interesting that within a flu virus resides its immunization, near poison oak grows the jewelweed, and within a snake's venom is its antivenom? Einstein said, "There is a solution within every problem. However, you can't solve a problem with the same mind that created the problem." In other words, you must think outside the box.

Now that you've named and claimed the issue the nightmare is revealing, you simultaneously have the exact formula for the antidote. By reframing and redirecting the most painful part of the dream, you transform the poison into medicine. In fact, sometimes I like to call redirected nightmares, such as Jenny's reframed dream in the previous section, "*right*-mares."

When you don't like the direction your dream is going, rewrite it! And if you are stuck in a nightmare and you feel you can't figure out how to turn it around, then *wake yourself up* in the dream. Look in the mirror, into the depth of your eyes, and remind yourself that you are an unlimited phenomenon. There are no periods, only commas in your story. If it is all made up, you might as well make up a story that is entertaining and liberating for you (and everyone else). Use your five senses to reenact your dream in your mind (or with your Dream Mastermind Group) from the perspective of being victorious (supported, appreciated, strengthened, empowered, respected, etc.). Exaggerate the scene in your mind's eye. The goal is to override the imprint left by the poison with the exact opposite quality that is the antidote.

Now that you've successfully redirected your venting dream—within the integrity of the dream—meditate on the new feeling tone that's emerged from your redirected dream, until your body feels dream alchemy settle in. You will know that you've successfully done this when you feel your breathing deepen, your heart open, your posture lengthen, and maybe even tears streaking your face, and a sense of clarity that accompanies redirection.

Identify the "alchemy word" that expresses the way you feel within your reframed dream. For example, Jenny felt "whole," whereas you may feel satiated, vindicated, free, liberated, empowered, ten feet tall, strong, gorgeous, grateful, wise, compassionate, or calm. Once you've chosen an alchemy word, repeat it silently to yourself, as you feel its medicinal effects reframing your awareness, shifting you from victim to victor, from tragic to triumphant, from shadow to illumined, and from beast to beauty.

Treat this feeling tone like a sacred touchstone you carry with you throughout your day. The entire hard drive of your mind's computer is being rewired. Once you allow this process to take place, the evidence of this newly embodied "you" will be inevitably, undeniably manifested in the third dimension.

Embodying Your Power

What if you were powerful beyond measure, but you've forgotten? Most of us have no idea that we are, in fact, powerful. And those who do have a clue as to how much power they actually have can often misuse it by misidentifying their power as being external, finite, and related to the material world of the ego. I believe the most important thing for us to embody is our power.

And once we do embody that power, I believe the next most important step is to become responsible for that power.

> *Most rarely align with their true power, because it seems illogical to them that there is power—power in relaxation, in letting go, in love, in joy, or in bliss. Most people do not understand their true power lies in releasing resistance—which is the only obstacle to their true power.*
>
> ABRAHAM/HICKS

The human comedy/tragedy is that we are these turbo-powerful beings that spend most of our time roaming the earth feeling disenfranchised, powerless, and small. We are, indeed, gods and goddesses (who have forgotten we are gods and goddesses) who have directorial input into how our lives play out.

Perhaps, because most of us (until now) didn't have the ability to properly, mindfully, and consciously own our power, it has been relegated to our blind spots and is thus used unconsciously. One thing I know is that when we take one step toward our dream, our dream takes ten steps toward us. In other words, all we need to do is a little bit of dreamwork in the morning to embody our power, and throughout the rest of the day the universe kicks in by giving us nudges, navigational direction, intuitive hits, and *aha*s galore. It's as if our willingness to move in the direction of our dream is the key to unleashing this phenomenal universal support.

It's so comical how power hungry we humans are. Okay, you may not think of it as power you are chasing, but consider that the power you lust for may be in the guise of money, fame, security, health, vitality, beauty, validation, opportunity, youth, love, or companionship. When we are asleep to who we are, we become such for-*get*-ful creatures. A telltale sign we've forgotten who we are is when our energy is about the business of *getting* something, *getting* someone, *getting* somewhere. In all our getting, we forget who we truly are and become like greyhounds chasing an artificial rabbit around and around the track.

What if Your Power Is Chasing You?

You've heard the saying "You can't hit a moving target." If you feel plagued by insecurity, then perhaps you have been elusive prey—bobbing and weaving your way through life in such a way that your power can never quite catch you. Think of your power like a stalker on the scent of an obsession—*you!*—always lurking in your blind spot, waiting for the right moment to leap out and have its way with you.

Dreamtime may be the only place you are at rest long enough for your power to get a good shot at you! I believe the reason so many people have "chasing" dreams/nightmares is because we, as a species, are radically cut off from our true power, by our own doing. That's good news: Because if we could cut ourselves off, then we can reconnect ourselves, too.

Think of yourself at the moment of your birth: a perfect, magnificent, precious child—irrevocably whole and complete. Throughout every trauma, moment of stress, or heartbreak, a part of you, like pieces of a puzzle, became disconnected.

Native Americans call the process of finding your lost pieces and putting them back together "Soul Retrieval." I believe our "chasing" dreams/nightmares are our missing puzzle pieces seeking to catch us in order to reconnect and restore us to our original form. We think the menace chasing us in our dreams is hell-bent on annihilating us, and perhaps to some degree that is true. Perhaps our power is seeking to annihilate our limited, flimsy, disempowered way of being, so that we can awaken to the beauty of our true selves. So the only thing that will be annihilated will be our egos and the mask of being a lacking, limping, shivering, quivering, and barely breathing human being.

When we face and embrace that which is chasing us (in dreams or in waking reality), we realize that which doesn't kill us makes us stronger, and that which does kill us transforms us. To illustrate this point, Michael Bernard Beckwith, founder of the Agape International Spiritual Center,[6] shares the following "chasing" dream:

> A few years prior to embarking upon my life as a minister, I had a series of dreams where three men were chasing me. Each night they would get a little closer. At one point they were very close, and I was going to wake myself up like I normally did. But this time I turned around and there was a small tent behind me, with a long line of people. The line was so long I couldn't even see the end of it, and I realized I knew everyone in this line. I thought to myself, "These men can't hurt me, because I have all these friends here. I started shouting for help and all the people turned their backs on me. Two of the men grabbed me and held me down as the third man plunged a knife into my heart. It was physically excruciating. I screamed . . . and I died.

"When I woke up from that dream I was surrounded by a presence I could only describe as 'Love Beauty,'" Michael Bernard Beckwith explains. "At the time, I was agnostic and the word *God* wasn't a part of my vocabulary. My whole life changed after that dream. I began to research what had happened to me; I began to study Eastern and Western mysticism; I began to meditate; I lost all my friends because they thought I freaked out. They were right. On some level I did freak out . . . in a good way. Dying in my dream marked the beginning, as an adult, of my pursuit of an awareness of oneness with the Presence."

As one who has studied with Michael Bernard Beckwith on and off over the past twenty years, I can attest to the fact that his dream wasn't the ending, but the beginning of him living his true purpose for being born. So, if you are killed in a dream, rejoice! It may be initiating you into a whole new dimension of the life that you came here to live!

Power Meditation

This meditation can be done anytime during the day but tends to be most effective in the moments bookending your sleep (right before sleep and upon awakening—after you write your dreams down in your dream journal!). To reap the benefits of this meditation I recommend you access it in any of the following ways:

- Read the following in a meditative way, slowly contemplating each sentence, breathing deeply with each thought, pausing to close your eyes to take in each element that resonates with you.

- Record yourself reading the meditation (slowly, allowing pauses between the phrases). Play your recording for yourself to enjoy in a relaxed environment with your eyes closed.

- Download the mp3 of this meditation from *www .KellySullivanWalden.com/meditations*

- Create a relaxed atmosphere for yourself where you won't be interrupted.

- Keep a journal and pen nearby to write down your *aha*s or insights stimulated by the meditation.

Take a few deep breaths, and as you do, let go of everything you think you know, everything you think you are striving for, hoping for, seeking to create, or influence. Just for now, as you breathe and exhale, surrender, wave the white flag, and let go. Let go of everything you are holding on to in any way, shape, or form.

Allow a violet flame to encircle your feet, and as this violet flame rises with each breath you take, feel it consume

your entire inner and outer vision. This violet flame trans-
mutes any energies that don't align with the highest frequency
of love. And let it go.

And now, feel the deep ease of knowing you can breathe
deeply and replace the energy the violet flame has removed.
Replace that energy with the sunlight of the spirit, love, intel-
ligence, guidance, and beauty that govern the universe. As
you drop into a deep feeling of relief, ease, and grace, feel as
though you are wrapped up in a billowing cloud, gently float-
ing across the sky, without a worry in the world.

You are now ready to come face-to-face with your true
power. Not the power based on external effects, but the true
power that comes from the center of the fire of creation. As
you breathe, feel a deep ease and peace, allow yourself to
come face-to-face with the Love Beauty of this universe that
is specifically yours. A great door opens and reveals the gifts
that belong to you, the love that is yours, the talents, and the
greatness.

Breathe deeply as you say yes to all this power, beauty,
love, brilliance, and gifts that are yours. Feel as though you've
stepped right into the center of the sun itself; feel the heat, the
radiance, the power, the strength, the confidence, and never-
ending goodness of the universe pulsating through you. With
each breath you are becoming comfortable with this power—
remembering it is natural to feel this level of vitality, clarity,
and thriving.

Think about an area of your life that you've felt a defi-
cit, a struggle, a lack of power. Envision yourself walking into
that situation, dealing with that person, or facing that chal-
lenge with this new level of power. Envision how the situa-
tion would be transformed with your newly embodied power.
Notice the situation shifting, altering, and morphing, like a

lucid dream in which you remember you have directorial input. See how the situation rights itself in such a way that everyone wins. Feel the energy shift as a result of your internal alchemy. Now do this same process for any other area of your life you experience a deficit in power.

Get the sense that you've resurrected, no longer relating to yourself in the same way. This is the "awakened" you who has been here all along but is now here for you and all to see. Your power no longer needs to hunt you down, because you have faced it and embraced it.

Give thanks to yourself for your willingness to embrace and embody the power that is rightly yours—and know that there's more where this comes from as you elevate from glory to greater glory along your dream life.

Questions for Contemplation

1. Describe a dream that you would like to embody. Write it out in as much detail as you can, with a particular emphasis on the feeling tone.

2. Meditate on the feeling tone of the dream. Once you've done this for a few minutes, describe your state of being (i.e., tingling, peaceful, energized, warm, glowing).

3. Where in your body do you feel the greatest concentration of energy?

4. Now that you are in the Embodiment of your wonderful dream, imagine that you've mastered this feeling and it is now your reference point. Describe the way you would carry this into your waking life.

5. Describe the impact this might have on your career, relationships, finances health, and spiritual connection.

If you want to make your dreams come true, the first thing you have to do is wake up.

J. M. Power

Chapter 6

Portal 4 —
A Is for *Activation*

All the good things in life have come from the world of visions and dreams. Someone entered the finer realms of life for a moment and brought back a treasure. The practical mind turned it to use and the world was richer and better than it was before.

CHRISTIAN D. LARSON

Activation: n. Derived from active. Meaning: to make active; cause to function or act. In physics, to render more reactive; excite: as in to activate a molecule; to induce radioactivity; to make active or capable of action.

Every Dream Requires Action

On a chilly London morning David Brown awoke with a bizarre series of numbers clearly etched in his mind. He rolled out of bed and wrote down what seemed like a phone number. Later in the day he found himself thinking about them; becoming a bit obsessed, he couldn't stop wondering what the number was for and what it could possibly mean. When he could no longer contain his curiosity, he summoned his courage and sent a text message to the mysterious number. On the receiving end of the text was his wife—or should I say *future* wife. The woman who received his text, whom he'd never met before, lived more than sixty miles away. Because David took his dream seriously and acted upon it, he met and later married Michelle, the woman of his dreams.[7]

I believe that every remembered nighttime dream requires some form of action in the waking world. The activation could simply be to give the "DDR"—the Daily Dream Report—to someone with whom you enjoy sharing your dreams, go on a bike ride, or look up an old high school friend on Facebook. You never know when the sharing of a dream will Activate a difference in your life and the life of the person you shared it with. What may seem insignificant to you might completely change the life of the person on the receiving end of the DDR.

In my experience, when we take action inspired from our dreamtime, it's as if we are telling our soul, "I'm paying attention to you." "You are important to me." "What else do you want me to know, do, or explore?" When our soul feels that it has someone to play with, it really begins to show up . . . and even show off! I find that with each dream activation I do, I feel that my level of confidence raises, not because of fly-by-night external forces, but because I feel connected to my soul and, thus, the core of the universe. As strange as it may sound, with every dream activation I do, it is as if I am simultaneously grounded and uplifted at the same time. As Abraham (as channeled through Esther Hicks) says, "When we are tuned in, tapped in, and turned on, life is sweet."

In other words, when you recognize when your dreams are "talking to you" about changes to make or actions to take in your waking life, dream activation increases the volume of your intuition and amplifies your ability to follow your dream clues toward greater confidence, intuition, and success in your waking life.

Drill Here!

When you get a strong feeling from your dream, it is a message from the universe to "drill here." I use that as a figure of speech meaning to explore and Activate the symbol, feeling, or situation that your dream revealed. However in the case of my friend Gini Gentry's dream, "drill here" couldn't have been more literal.

Gini moved to the high desert of New Mexico to get away from the hustle and bustle of big-city living. What she loved best about living in the desert was the ability to see the stars at night and to breathe in clean air all day long.

What she liked least, however, was the lack of water. For the first nine years she lived on her property, the water was a trickle from a tiny spring. Every summer she was profoundly careful parsing out the water for bathing and washing dishes, using the minimum amount. Occasionally her supply would run dry. She would then have to drive thirty-five miles into town to buy water to put in a storage tank. As you might imagine, the storage tank was cumbersome and heavy, and driving in to town to fill it was something to do only in an extreme situation.

On her ninth summer on her property, she was in a crisis for three reasons:

1. It was hotter than normal.

2. Her trickle had diminished to a drip.

3. She didn't have the money to dig a well. She knew a lot of people in the area who'd spent tens of thousands of dollars digging for phantom wells that came up disappointingly dry.

"I didn't have the finances on hand to gamble with it," said Gini.

She prayed for guidance, for answers, for help. And in her own way, she set a powerful Dream Declaration. The dream she received wasn't an elaborate one, but one that made *all* the difference.

> In my dream I'm walking on my property behind a huge rock formation. I get the strongest feeling about this place . . . and I suddenly know this is the place to drill for water.

Gini was filled with such a sense of knowing that she a brought in a "water witch" (a person skilled in the use of dowsing rods and intuition to find water), whose dowsing rods practically threw him off his feet, spinning wildly as he approached the area she dreamed about.

Not long after that, Gini paid to drill for water. To her joy, she no longer has to rely on a little trickle, because she now has *water flowing at fifty gallons a minute*—and it's been flowing that way for the past thirteen years! Now Gini's ranch is the place her neighbors come to when they run out of water!

Because of her dream and the discovery of water on her property, Gini was able to establish her land as the retreat center she had always dreamed of. Garden of the Goddess (*www.GiniGentry.com*) is the place where she and her former teaching partner, Don Miguel Ruiz (author of *The Four Agreements*) led numerous retreats. It remains a thriving oasis where Gini leads her own workshops and private sessions. In fact, for a year, my husband and I lived on this amazing property and enjoyed every drop of its delicious water.

Save Others

Julie awoke with heart palpitations from a disturbing dream about a man tragically hurt in a tractor accident. Upon awakening Julie scratched her head and uttered the famous phrase many people say when they don't immediately understand the message of their dream: "I had the strangest dream!" Like a good dream mastery student, Julie remained connected with her dream despite the fact she could not reconcile how to make sense of it or what to do with it. On this typical California morning, Julie took her cup of freshly brewed coffee with her to retrieve the newspaper from her front porch. All was as it should be: The sun was shining, the neighborhood was waking up, parents were walking their children to school—except for one thing. Across the street from Julie's house was *a man digging up the neighbor's lawn with a tractor!*

Julie's jaw, newspaper, and cup of coffee dropped to the porch as she realized this was the man on a tractor from her dream. If she lived in the country, or even in a partially rural area, this might not have been such a shock. However, in the twenty years she'd lived in this neighborhood, she had never seen anyone on a tractor, nor had she ever dreamed of a tractor. She took a deep breath, and against the protest of her ego, in her coffee-splattered bathrobe and slippers, she crossed the street and approached the man.

"Excuse me, sir. I know this might sound crazy, but last night I dreamed of a man in a tractor accident. I'm not trying to scare you, but perhaps by me telling you this you will be a bit more careful today than you otherwise would be."

The man looked at her as if she had just escaped from the loony bin and reassured her with an uncomfortable laugh that he would be careful.

When she came home from work late that afternoon, the tractor was gone, and in its place was her neighbor. Julie crossed the street and asked if everything had gone okay that day, to which the neighbor smirked, "Everything went fine. The worker didn't fall off the tractor, if that's what you were wondering about."

Julie's ego was a bit scuffed by the interchange, but her soul felt satisfied in knowing that by taking action on behalf of her dream, she may have prevented an accident from happening. *"Vale la pena!"* she thought, "It's worth the pain."

Save Your Life

The vision must be followed by the venture. It is not enough to stare up the steps—we must step up the stairs.

VANCE HAVNER

There's a saying among the Iroquois, "Everything happens first in dreams." There is another saying, "Pain is necessary, but suffering is optional." By paying attention to dreams and taking action, as Julie did, you can avoid (and help others to avoid) unnecessary suffering.

The following dream series also illustrates the power of dream Activation (albeit a bit more dramatically) and its ability to not only be life enhancing but also unquestionably lifesaving.

Just like millions of women over forty, Kathleen O'Keefe-Kanavos dutifully went through the motions of getting her yearly mammogram. Even though she was accustomed to getting a clean bill of health, she couldn't help but sigh in relief when her doctor told her, "Your report shows you are a healthy woman, Kathleen. Keep doing what you are doing. We'll see you next year."

In spite of the great news, that night Kathleen had the following dream:

> A hooded Franciscan monk came to me and admonished in a very clear voice, "Go back to the doctor. You are very sick. You have cancer. It is right here in your breast." He pointed to the underside of my left breast. I touched my breast and felt a tiny lump."

Kathleen woke up that morning upset by her dream. She had a mile-long list of things to do that day, so she shrugged off the dream the way the sun shoos away a dark cloud, and she charged headlong into her busy day. Later that night, she and her husband were having a romantic evening. Soaking in a warm, candlelit bubble bath and sipping Champagne with soft music in the background, Kathleen and her husband began to get amorous. Without getting into the details, let's just say Kathleen's husband was lathering her body and began caressing her breasts—when abruptly he stopped and blurted, "What's this lump?"

"What lump?"

"Right here," he said touching a spot on the underside of her left breast.

Like an ice cold shower, Kathleen's dream from the previous night came rushing through her mind, and she knew she had to take action.

The next day she went to the doctor and told him about her dream, showed him the lump and requested another mammogram.

The doctor replied, "Kathleen, if this tiny lump was more than a fibroid tumor, it would have showed up in the mammogram. You had blood tests, and everything came back fine. I think you are taking this dream a bit too seriously. You should be happy to be so healthy. Enjoy your clean bill of health. Believe me, there are many people who I wish I could say this to."

Kathleen wanted to believe the doctor (who wouldn't want to believe such good news?) but, at the risk of looking like a hypochondriac, she knew she needed another mammogram. In fact, she had *three* more mammograms and two more blood tests from two other doctors, all of whom came back saying the same thing: "Kathleen, there is nothing wrong with you. If you'd like to schedule another exam in six months, you're welcome to. Until then, go home and enjoy your life!"

She did as the doctors ordered. She figured she had honored her dream by taking additional tests, and eventually she got back to the business of enjoying her life . . . until a couple weeks later the monk came to call again in her dream:

> This time he handed me a white feather and said, "Go back to your doctor, without an appointment. Fence with the doctor verbally and convince him you need exploratory surgery on this spot. While you are 'fencing' with him, in your mind's eye, see yourself holding this feather, and you will win."

By the way, Kathleen lives in Cape Cod and her doctor's office is in Boston. These trips are no easy jaunt for her. At this point her husband was getting frustrated and the doctors were exasperated, yet she knew on a deep level that she needed to honor the message of her dream. She did as the monk instructed. She held her ground while fencing with the invisible feather, and despite her doctor's intense resistance, he acquiesced and scheduled her surgery.

Immediately following the surgery the doctor told her in an apologetic, somber voice, "Pathology didn't like what they saw. What we thought was a fibroid tumor is actually stage II cancer."

Her next surgery was scheduled right away and they found the cancer had already spread into her lymph nodes. Had she waited six months later for her next mammogram—as the doctors suggested—it would have been too late.

Over the next five years, Kathleen experienced this phenomenon three more times, leading to a double mastectomy, which she accounts in detail in her memoir *Surviving Cancerland* (*www.survivingcancerland.com*).

At present, Kathleen is cancer-free, living a full and passionate life with her husband (award-winning author Peter Kanavos.) She has had a genuine, clean bill of health and has not heard nor seen her dream monk in years. She often thinks about the white feather the monk gave her in her dream.

"Every time I envision holding that feather," she says, "I feel peaceful, powerful, and connected to a higher realm, one that gives me strength and a true sense of confidence. If it wasn't for that dream and for that little, white feather, I wouldn't be alive right now. When I think about it I am flooded with gratitude—gratitude for the dream and gratitude for having the audacity to act upon it."

Here's another dreamer who Activated his dream in his waking life and is alive and well to tell the tale.

Toby, a tall, muscular man's man had always prided himself on physical strength and success as one of the music industry's most talented alternative rock producers. Toby had been recording and arranging head-banging, gut-wrenching, soul-splitting music with screaming vocals for so long that he never would have imagined it could penetrate his body armor. Seemingly out of nowhere, Toby's right eyelid began to droop and a numb, burning sensation began to permeate the center of his skull, indicating severe nerve damage in his upper spinal area.

He visited numerous doctors of both Eastern and Western practices and not one could tell him what was wrong with him. Just as hopelessness and despair had almost entirely engulfed him, he began to have the following recurring dream *on a nightly basis:*

> I enter a large Mediterranean-type building in a country setting.
> There is an engraving over the arches of the doorway that reads
> HOME TO ALL WHOLENESS AND WELL-BEING. I approach the blond
> receptionist. Behind her, there are numerous colored hallways.
> She greets me: "Hello, Mr. Wright," and indicates a color fol-
> lowed by a number to signify my room assignment (i.e., "You're
> in room yellow 23 today."). I follow her instructions by proceed-
> ing to the appropriate colored hallway, then on to the assigned
> room number.

From side-mounted speakers I listen to sound waves pulsating at different frequencies blended in a way that promotes the restoration of my mind and body.

Upon awakening, Toby's dreams compelled him to dive deep into researching sound healing (quite the departure, as you might imagine, from the guitar-gnashing sounds he'd been accustomed to). Because of this series of dreams, Toby was inspired to explore producing the kinds of tones, frequencies, pulsations, modulations, and harmonics experienced in his dreams. Lucky for him, as a music producer, every bit of equipment he could possibly need was at his disposal. He began creating healing tones for himself, and within a short period of time, without medication, Toby's symptoms dissolved!

This alone would make for a groundbreaking Dream Activation success story, but there's more. Toby has since produced sixteen healing music CDs and he has helped many people to "mysteriously" feel better and, in some cases, recover entirely from their illnesses. The financial cherry on top of this musical hot fudge sundae is that a top Las Vegas casino and spa just licensed his sound-healing CDs. If this keeps up, Toby, one of rock's most successful producers, will be synonymous with healing, all because of his dream (and his dream Activation!).

But, wait, there's more. Just when you thought dreams couldn't get more extraordinary, the following is another example of Dream Activation that had an enormously medicinal—not to mention life-changing—outcome.

I spend most of my days either facilitating dream therapy (coaching) sessions, speaking at conferences about dreams, or returning as many emails and Facebook requests for dream interpretation as I can. One seemingly ordinary day in my unordinary life, I received an email request for a dream interpretation:

Dear Kelly,

I recently had this dream that I would love your help with understanding:

In my dream I am suspended in a billowing white light and though I am alone, I have a sense that someone (or something) is with me. I suddenly feel an amazing power lift me higher. I hear in the distance encouraging words, and as I listen to what sounds like words being spoken that explode into a resonance that gets louder and louder, it completely takes me over. I feel peace all around me as the words become clearer: "Smile . . . Smile big . . . Smile as big as you can!" These words continue for what seems like hours and I am in pure bliss.

I'd love to hear what you think it means!

Smiling Big,

Diane

I responded:

Dear Diane,

Usually our angels or guides wait for us to come to them . . . but in this case, I believe they made an exception to the rule and are reaching out to you. My hunch about your dream is that it is a prescription being written to you by your higher power to smile, smile big.

This is one of those dreams that requires a minimum of interpretation and a maximum of meditation. In fact, I suggest you take the prescription (from your dream) as if it was medicine, by simply contemplating this feeling tone of floating within that "billowing sensation," and smiling as big as you can, as often as you can, until that feeling becomes "ordinary." Think of this feeling as a touchstone to anchor you in a place of awakening to the truth of your magnificence.

Also smiling big,

Kelly

Eight months later I received this email from Diane:

Kelly!

Thank you for your response to my dream inquiry nearly a year ago. In case you don't remember me, I am the "Smile Big" lady. At the time I sent you my dream I didn't mention to you that I had just been diagnosed with a rare brain cancer (a schwannoma tumor) and my life was in utter chaos. However, my dream came to my rescue. After I shared it with you, I took your advice and have continued to meditate on the billowing sensation and the incredible peaceful way my dream made me feel.

The reason I'm writing you today is because I just got back from the doctor and he said it is a "miracle" . . . my tumor seems to have disappeared! It's as if it "fell off." No one can believe it. All I know is that I feel great and I have a new lease on life. I know the dream by itself was powerful (like medicine) but it was the work I did with the dream (like taking the medicine) that made all the difference. I feel like a new woman . . . one who smiles big . . . and has much to smile about!

Smiling Big,
Diane

As Kathleen, Toby, and Diane all said, their dreams were healing unto themselves. However, when they took the time, energy, and determination to *Activate* them in real life, the real healing kicked in.

> *If we deny the wishes of the soul, then soul will become disgusted and withdraw vital energy from our lives. We'll become prone to illness and misfortune. Following the secret wishes of our soul, on the other hand, can return us to the natural path of our energies and restore vitality, good health, and good fortune.*
>
> ROBERT MOSS

Get Rich (Or at Least Richly Enhance Your Life)

Perhaps at this point, you can see that your dreams are not to be taken lying down. In addition to dream Activation being a key to helping you survive more powerfully in your life, dream activation can also help you thrive. In other words, the potential in dream Activation is that it can exponentially grease the wheels of your career, in some cases alter the entire trajectory of your life, and—while you're at it—enhance the lives of many people.

In the introduction to this book I mention a list of people who brought the brilliance of their dream into three dimensions and altered the world. All of these life-altering, mind-bending, and world-shifting contributions took place because of the principal of Activation. These people did not leave their dreams on their pillow. They knew their dreams weren't over just because they woke up. Instead these dreamers did the work to transfer their dream wisdom from the sleep state into the waking world, and thus their lives were altered for the better.

In his mega-best-selling book *Think and Grow Rich*, Napoleon Hill interviewed and researched more than five hundred of the most successful people in history to determine what common attributes they shared that allowed them to create prosperous and purpose-driven lives. He found all the people he interviewed had one thing in common. Every single one of the individuals he profiled in *Think and Grow Rich* recognized their intuition as a powerful resource and honored it by deliberately developing it (more about that on page 209).

Did you know that *enhanced intuition is one of the primary benefits of dreamwork?* The second benefit of dreamwork is enhanced creativity. And last, but certainly not least, the third benefit of dreamwork is a stronger connection with one's spiritual source, which leads to a heightened self-esteem and confidence.

There are thousands of examples of people whose dreams enhanced their intuition, creativity, and spirituality. Here are a few examples of those who were also richly rewarded by their dream recall and subsequent activation.

On My Nerves

Dr. Otto Loewi dreamed about two frog hearts placed in a laboratory separate from one another, the first with its nerves, the second without. In his dream he had a hunch that it was not the nerves that influenced the heart directly, but the chemical substance that was transmitted between the nerves. Upon awakening Dr. Loewi conducted an experiment that proved the theory of chemical transmission (later identified as acetylcholine) of the nerve impulse. In 1936, Dr Loewi was awarded the Nobel Prize for his discovery.

Banting and the Beast

Prior to the discovery of insulin, doctors prescribed patients suffering from diabetes a low-sugar diet. Though it helped to extend their lives, it could not save them. While seeking the cause of diabetes, Dr. Frederick Banting had a dream instructing him to tie up the pancreas (surgically ligate it to stop the flow of nourishment) of a diabetic dog and pay close attention to its production of insulin. Banting Activated his dream and did what it instructed. He discovered the disproportionate balance between sugar and insulin. This breakthrough led to his next dream that revealed to him *how* to develop insulin as a drug to treat the disease. Because of his dream activation, in 1923 Banting was awarded the Nobel Prize in Physiology and Medicine.

A Stitch in Time

In his waking life, inventor Elias Howe was struggling to figure out how to make a needle cut through a piece of cloth on the sewing machine he was creating. He decided to "sleep on it," and his dream came to the rescue:

> I was taken prisoner by a group of natives. They were dancing around with spears. As they were moving around me, I noticed their spears all had holes near their tips.

Even though he was frightened when he awoke, he realized that by placing a hole at the tip of the needle, the thread could be caught after pushing through the cloth. He promptly changed his design to Activate the dream idea and found it worked—and beat Singer to the finish line.[8]

Embrace Your Inner Frankenstein

During the rainy summer of 1816, at the ripe old age of eighteen, Mary Shelley dreamed of "a pale student of unhallowed arts kneeling beside the thing he had put together. I saw the hideous phantasm of a man stretched out, and then, on the working of some powerful engine, show signs of life, and stir with an uneasy, half vital motion. Frightful must it be; for *supremely* frightful would be the effect of any human endeavor to mock the stupendous mechanism of the Creator of the world."

With the urgings of Lord Byron, Mary Shelley wrote her dream and expanded it into the book *Frankenstein,* now considered a landmark work of Romantic and Gothic literature, as well as one of the first works of science fiction.

Oil Well in His Own Backyard

In September 1937, the Kuwait Oil Company was unsuccessfully drilling in Bahra until one night, Colonel Harold Dickson dreamed of a beautiful woman buried in an underground tomb. In his dream he rescued the damsel in distress, fed her, and gave her warm clothes. To thank him, the beauty led her hero to an ancient sidr tree, growing alone in the desert. She sat beneath the tree while he fought off hostile men to defend her. Upon awakening, with the help of a local Bedouin dream interpreter, Colonel Dickson discovered the exact location of this particular tree and shared it with the sheikh of Kuwait. The sheikh commanded drilling operations to begin in Al-Burqan, the area near the lonely sidr tree. Within a few months he hit a gusher that became one of the richest oil discoveries in history.[9]

Birds of a Feather

One night Richard Bach dreamed of a rebellious seagull who wanted to explore beyond the boundaries of what his flock thought was appropriate. This feathered outcast hooked Bach's attention and Bach decided to write about it. Once the book was written, it was promptly rejected by every major New York publisher on the basis that "no one would be interested in a silly story about a self-expressed seagull." After years of rejection and crushing financial hardships, Bach was about to give up. As his car was being repossessed, he walked out into his front yard and pulled out a letter from his mailbox. When he saw it was from an editor at Macmillan Publishers, he assumed it would be yet another rejection letter to add to his towering pile. However, this publisher (who had already rejected the book) said she would like to take a risk on it . . . and the rest is history. By the end of 1972, over a million copies of *Jonathan Livingston Seagull* were in print, and it reached the top of the *New York Times* Best-Seller List, where it remained for thirty-eight weeks. In 1972 and 1973 the book topped the *Publishers Weekly* list of best-selling novels in the United States, and it remains a classic in libraries and in schools to this day, all because a little seagull made a dreamtime appearance . . . and Richard Bach took note.

Forty Thousand Shares

Bernard M. Wagner, MD, had a recurring dream about an obscure biotech stock called ICOS. He bought about forty thousand shares of ICOS, using his entire life savings, for around $4 a share. When he sold the shares in 1998, they were worth $28 each, which works out to over $1 million in profits.

Get a Grip

Golf legend Jack Nicklaus attributes his success in part to a dream he had in which he was gripping a golf club differently than he normally did. In real life he'd been having trouble collapsing his right arm and taking the club head away from the ball. But in his dream, with this new grip, he was swinging perfectly. He practiced his "dream grip" in real life and it worked. "I feel kind of foolish admitting it," said Nicklaus, "but it really happened in a dream."[10]

Pioneering Pandora

One morning in 1995, award-winning film director James Cameron awoke breathless from an epic dream about a land called Pandora. In this rainforest-like dreamscape the people were an enlightened hybrid of aliens and humans, speaking a language that was foreign yet understandable to him. Luckily for James Cameron (and *Avatar* fans worldwide), he respected his dream world and took copious notes. Ten years and several technological quantum leaps later, Cameron's dusty dream notes served as a travelogue for the entire production . . . a world that Cameron had already visited. *Avatar*, made with a $250 million budget (the biggest movie budget in history), was released in the 2009 holiday season and has grossed more than $1.7 billion and counting.[11]

Unsightly Cell Phone Towers

Now here is someone I doubt you've heard of, but once you read his story perhaps you'll think of his dream contribution every time you see a cell phone tower. John, a gentleman from one of my dreamworkshops, reported dreaming of a beautiful palm tree sprouting out of a cell phone tower. Upon awakening, he jotted down his vision. He has since patented his design to the tune of several million dollars. His "fake tree" designs now cover up those less-than-aesthetically-pleasing cell phone towers sprouting up across the nation.

Benevolent, Honest, and Sparkly Vampire

Stephenie Meyer was a stay-at-home mom who dabbled with writing from time to time and was certainly not into vampire stories at all. However, one night, she had the following dream:

> Two people are having an intense conversation in a meadow in the woods. One of these people is just your average girl. The other person is this fantastically beautiful, sparkly vampire. They are discussing the difficulties inherent in the facts that (a) they are falling in love with each other while (b) the vampire is particularly attracted to the scent of her blood and is having a difficult time restraining himself from killing her immediately.

This dream was so vivid that Stephenie began to write what became the mega-hit *Twilight*. This led to the next book in the Twilight series . . . then the next . . . then the next . . . and the rest is history. To date she has sold more than 116 million copies in fifty countries, and the movie version of the last story in the saga, *Breaking Dawn 2*, broke box office records by making $577.7 million its first week.

We are all blessed that Stephenie Meyer, "Cell Phone Tower" John, James Cameron, Richard Bach, Jack Nicklaus, Bernard M. Wagner, Colonel Harold Dickson, Mary Shelley, Elias Howe, Dr. Frederick Banting, and Dr. Otto Loewi (among others) did not shrug off their nighttime bursts of genius as "just a dream."

Their activations and subsequent results show that dreams can come bearing treasures. I pray that this inspires you to never again take your dreams for granted, but rather, starting now, to honor and Activate them in your waking life.

I know the skeptic in you may be wondering, "Are the aforementioned dreams common? Don't those kinds of dreams happen once in a lifetime, and only to a few people?"

Yes, they are special, and yes they do happen to ordinary people like you and me. I believe as we evolve as a species, these dream experiences will become more frequent. In the meantime, while you await your life altering, multi-million-dollar, multi-platinum dream, consider that the way you do dreamwork on ordinary days will help you build the habits and the psychological/spiritual muscles to behold and Activate your extraordinary dreams when they grace your dreamscape. By training yourself to pay attention to "ordinary" dreams (as if there really were such a thing), you will be in position to not shrug it off as *just a dream* when it come down the pike. Prepare to catch it, Activate it, and then celebrate the 3-D results.

If you have built castles in the air, your work need not be lost; that is where they should be. Now put the foundations under them.

Henry David Thoreau

SleepWorking

Invention is 1 percent inspiration and 99 percent perspiration.

Thomas Edison

Regarding dream Activation, Thomas Edison is the poster child. If he was correct that invention is 99 percent perspiration, then where does the 1 percent inspiration come from? If he were alive to answer that question, I'd bet he would say, "It's all in your dreams."

Edison had a love/hate relationship with sleep. Instead of getting a full eight hours a night, Edison would sleep approximately four hours and take catnaps in the afternoon. Sometimes he would stop in the midst of grappling with an invention and, with a specific question on his mind, doze off while sitting upright in a chair. He would place a weight in the palm of each hand, and a plate on the floor beneath each hand. He knew when he heard the clamor of the weight hitting the plate he had entered into sleep and the dream portal was open. He would then write down whatever dream wisp he could catch or whatever thought was passing through the sky of his mind. More often than not, he would find the dream wisp to be the answer to his question, or at least a step in the right direction. Not only did this process minimize some of his 99 percent perspiration, but it led to more than one thousand patents!

According to research by the Loughborough University Sleep Research Centre, "Humans function best when they sleep twice a day: the main one at night and the second in the afternoon. Their research shows that short naps can improve stamina and concentration."[12] So, if you get a little sleepy during the afternoon and find it a challenge to stay focused on the task at hand, don't reach for a Red Bull to power your way through the day. Tell your boss that even doctors now agree a short nap during this low-energy time can be highly productive, especially if you incubate your dreams with a work-related question. Companies that intend to increase productivity and become leaders in their respective fields would be well advised to *encourage* employees to take *power naps* in the middle of their shifts while contemplating issues/challenges at work in order to derive solutions beyond the grasp of the limited, logical mind.

Let's unpack this phenomenon of *SleepWorking* a bit more. In addition to it being something that happens deliberately during a midafternoon nap, it is also when you bring your work to bed with you. These work-related dreams come bearing their own set of benefits—and challenges. Some consider SleepWorking dreams a boring and frustrating rehash of the day's events, because they often are an extension of the people, places, and events from their daily lives. In these dreams you are tying up loose ends from the office or rehearsing ways to resolve a conversation or issue that went awry.

LeeAnn, a television producer friend of mine complained to me in the green room before I went on air: "I am constantly working, all day, all night—and even in my dreams! I can't get a break! I would love to be one of those people who have wild, fantastic, and romantic dream adventures in exotic locales. No! My dreams include producing our show, texting, meetings, sending and receiving emails, and being on the phone with the people I work with all day!"

LeeAnn is right; our SleepWorking dreams are not the most mystical or fantastically romantic dreams known to humankind. However, what SleepWorking dreams lack in fantasy they more than make up for in their ability to be practical in the light of day. The primary function of our SleepWorking dreams is to give us a jump on what is pressing in our immediate waking reality and to assist our subconscious to digest the bazillion message units we are exposed to all day. In fact, it may be LeeAnn's SleepWorking dreams that helped her to be nominated for an Emmy Award.

Canadian newspaper *The Globe and Mail* polled 7,600 people in 2008 and discovered that 53 percent of the people in the study reported frequent work-related dreams. Staples Inc. polled three hundred small-business owners and discovered that more than half of them reported having work-related dreams. Interestingly but not surprising, 70 percent of the people polled by Staples Inc. reported acting on their work-related dreams in the light of day.[13]

As tedious as these dreams may seem, they can give us a tremendous advantage, like eyes in the back of our head or a rehearsal before a play. Our SleepWorking dreams are unsung heroes helping us solve relationship issues, money conundrums, and solutions to health challenges we overlook in our waking life. Is it any wonder before making a major decision we say, "Let me sleep on it"? This is one of the smartest things we can do.

"I had no clue what I wanted to do with my life," Christy Ann Conlin reflects.[14] "It was 1993, I was a file clerk for a firm in Ottawa, Canada, and I was miserable. But I had no idea what to do. Until one night, I had the strangest dream:

> I am Madonna's file clerk. As I work in this dusty office, this amazing star (who I never was a huge fan of in real life) shared with me stories of her secrets for success. She told me that her greatest achievements were due to her ability to aspire beyond the ordinary.

Within a couple of weeks, Christy, who had never been a writer, began writing stories. She enrolled in a creative writing class and soon after earned a master's degree in fine arts from the University of British Columbia. Shortly thereafter, Christy landed a publishing deal with Doubleday for her book *Heave*, which soon became a national best seller. Christy thanks the Material Girl to this day for taking the time from her touring schedule to make a personal appearance in her dream and thus changing her life in a very material way.

Christy's dream story illustrates the following important points:

- If you have a question about your career or its decision, formulate a specific question, and think about it prior to sleep.

- Pay attention to your dreams, even if they seem abstract and appear unrelated to your question.

- If a celebrity makes an appearance in your work-related dream, consider that they are revealing insight on an issue that demands attention. They may also be shining a spotlight on hidden resources essential to your real-life drama.

- When a star enters your dream scene, ask yourself, "What is this celebrity known for? What larger-than-life quality are they emblematic of?" Your dream celeb may very well be revealing aspects of yourself to face and embrace so that you, too, may step confidently into the spotlight of your life.

- Take action on your dream and Activate its power into your waking reality.

Give Me a Break!

For those of you who have been deluged with SleepWorking dreams and are praying for a flight of fantasy type of dream, here's my recommendation:

- If there is a pressing matter happening at work, journal about it prior to bedtime (or write a list of what you will do to deal with it in the morning). Set that list aside (keep it far from your bedroom).

- Read a book about something or someone that tantalizes your imagination and takes it on a ride to a place that has nothing to do with your waking reality.

- Keep your cell phone and laptop (all work-related electronics) out of the bedroom, or at least covered with fabric.

- Download my sweet dreams meditation, and listen to it as you drift off to sleep, from: *www.kellysullivanwalden.com/meditations*

Activating Dreams into Your Waking Life

When one tugs at a single thing in nature, we find it attached to the rest of the world.

JOHN MUIR

As I mentioned in chapter 3, just as the folks at Harvard discovered, your dreams don't have to resemble actual guidance that makes sense. So at the very minimum, by simply maintaining a connection with your remembered dreams and allowing them to color the background of your thinking, you will be better off in your waking life. However, here are some things you can do to raise the bar:

1. Each morning, after writing your dreams in your journal, pick one element from your dream and meditate on it. For example you might explore in detail the feel of your dream lover's lips, the wind in your hair as the car sped through traffic in an exhilarating dream car chase, or your departed grandmother's all-knowing look in your dream encounter with her. *One dream detail can ensure you are deeply connected to the world of your dream and thus benefit from its guidance and genius throughout the day.*

2. Share it with someone, or at least write it in your own dream journal.

3. Carry the feeling tone with you as you go to work, drive the carpool, go to the store, and go about your daily round. For example, whenever there is a break between activities (i.e., waiting in line at the grocery store or sitting in bumper-to-bumper traffic), direct your attention to your remembered dream and allow it to color your thoughts and even inform your actions.

The SADDLE Dream Interpretation Formula

Thus far in this chapter we've explored the benefits of dream recall, sleeping on the job, SleepWorking, and dream Activation even in the face of *not* knowing what the dream means. Now it's time to up the ante and explore what happens when you spend a few minutes in the morning running a dream or two through the SADDLE dream interpretation formula. I find this practice to be effective in helping mine deeper levels of gold within each dream. SADDLE stands for *symbol, association, dream dictionary, life experience,* and *emotions.*

In my book *I Had the Strangest Dream . . .: The Dreamer's Dictionary for the 21st Century,* I outline a six-step dream interpretation that is similar to this one. However, as is the case with living and learning, this SADDLE formula is new and improved (think "Dream Interpretation Formula 2.0".)

The SADDLE formula came to me one day during a live interview, in response to a series of questions a radio show host asked. I must have heard questions like his a thousand times, but something snarky (I'm not normally snarky) bit its way through me. The interview went something like this:

Host: "Why don't dreams make sense? Why are they so strange and weird? If they really do have important messages for us, then why don't they just spell it out so we can understand them?"

Me: "It sounds as though you think your dreams should behave like a domesticated house pet—like they are something cute and fluffy that should sit, stay, or roll over when you snap your fingers. What if your dreams are wilder than that? What if they are more like a fire-breathing dragon than a docile house pet? Your dreams won't be tamed like your dog. If you truly want a relationship with your dreams, then treat them like the powerful dragon (like the "ikran" in James Cameron's movie *Avatar*).

"Give up the expectation that they will come down and meet you on the ground floor. Instead, be willing to rise to a higher level, learn to speak their language, follow their lead, and go where they lead. In essence, if you show your dreams the respect they deserve, conduct your life in such a way as to accommodate their needs (proper attention, sleep, diet, and adherence to your intuitive-soul-dream messages), you will in effect raise your consciousness to a higher vibration. As you do this, your dreams will become your greatest ally. They will invite you to *SADDLE* up and have the ride of your life, night after night. And as a by-product of this practice, you will become more confident, fearless, intuitive, insightful, shamanic, powerful, and a force to be reckoned with, in all your daily affairs . . . and beyond."

The host of the radio show looked at me as if *I* was the fire-breathing dragon, but I think he got it. He's asked me back as a regular guest, so I think my *snarkiness* didn't singe him too much!

Why *Are* Our Dreams So Strange?

If I wasn't feeling so snarky (don't you love that word?) a more scientific response to his question, "Why are our dreams so strange?" might have been the following:

Modern research has been able to scan the brain during sleep and dreaming, particularly during REM (rapid eye movement) sleep, where our eyes flutter beneath our eyelids as if we are watching the dream. These periods occur five or six times per night, usually for twenty to forty minutes. What science has discovered is that while we are asleep and dreaming, our whole brain doesn't fall asleep, but certain brain centers turn off, while others turn on. *One of the reasons why our dreams are so bizarre is because during sleep and dreaming, our brain centers that control logic and rational thinking (as well as the regions governing our motor skills) are inactive.*

But the parts of our brain that *are active* include our limbic system—which is the area of the brain that regulates emotion and memory. The job of our limbic system is to help us process our unresolved emotions and make sense of the events of the day. The limbic system even helps us make sense of our history, including past emotions and memories that have been unresolved.

Carl Jung was right when he said that dreams were about the unfinished business of the day.

The part of the brain with which we see our dreams is not the visual cortex through our eyes, but the area surrounding it called the association cortex. What this means is that all the things we see in our dreams are based on our own personal associations with the feelings and thoughts being processed.

So, "Why are our dreams so strange?"

It is because what we are seeing in our dreams are *pictures of our thoughts and feelings.* And we all know our feelings aren't bound by logic or rational thinking!

Saddle Dream Interpretation

Now, let's see if we can approach our wild, emotional dreams with a hint of logic, for the purpose of decoding our dreams.

1. On a blank sheet of paper or in your journal, write the word *SADDLE* across the top of a blank page:

   S   A   D   D   L   E

2. Beneath each letter fill in the information that relates to your dream as follows:

   S **(symbol):** What are the major symbols in your dream?

   A **(association):** What are your associations with these symbols?

   DD **(dream dictionary):** Cross-reference it with a book of symbols or a dream dictionary (i.e., *I Had the Strangest Dream . . . : The Dreamer's Dictionary for the 21st Century*) to see if it can fill in the gaps to give you a broader, more archetypal understanding.

   L **(life experience):** Is there any part of your dream that seems to directly tie in to what is happening lately in waking life?

   E **(emotions):** What are the major feelings/emotions/energies present in your dream?

   For example, Olivia had the following dream:

   I dreamed I was disembarking a cruise ship and once I hit dry land I realized I left my purse and little dog behind in my room. I awoke feeling panicked.

   This is how she decoded the message of her dream in her dream journal:

S (symbol)	A (association)	DD (dream dictionary)	L (life)	E (emotions)
• disembark • cruise ship • dry land • purse (abandoned) • puppy (abandoned)	• switching gears from fun to work mode • cruising, enjoying myself • practical reality • money issues • best friend	• Exit: completion, end of a cycle, time for change, transition • cruise ship: leisure, time to cruise, take it easy with relation*ship* • earth: grounded, practical • purse: *purse*-onal power, identity, self-worth, money issues • puppy: innocent, playful, instinctual aspect of self	• I've been struggling lately over issues of caretaking my ailing mother versus taking care of my own well-being. • In life and in relationships I tend to go to extremes, either I'm being a martyr, or extremely selfish—out of reaction.	• My overall feelings I recall from this dream are panic, loss, and worry.

3. Once you've written this down, read it all together, one column at a time, beginning with the *S* column, working your way to the *A*, to the *DD*, to the *L*, and ending with the *E* column. At this point you will most likely be getting some clarity about what message your dream is trying to send. Take note of the inevitable *aha*s that come from doing this.

For example, this is how Olivia interpreted her dream:

I need to learn to disembark (switch gears) from fun to work mode. I need to end this cycle I've been stuck in, and it's time for change; I can't take care of everyone else (i.e., my mother) and leaving myself out to dry. Perhaps if I could learn to cruise a bit more in my life and take (even just a little) time to enjoy myself, I could still tend to all the earthbound things that need to get done while not sacrificing my own purse-onal power. Maybe then I'd enjoy life more and—who knows—maybe have the energy (of a puppy) to get more of the practical things I need to get done.

As you learned in the previous Portal, if you have a dream like Olivia's that leaves you feeling less than empowered, then you can reenter your dream (see page 104) and redirect your dream to an exalted conclusion.

For example, in Olivia's redirected dream, she envisioned retrieving her purse and her dog and safely bringing everyone and everything important to her back to dry land. Once she did this she felt the gift of the dream was showing her how life might cruise along more gracefully if she integrated her sense of worth (purse) and playfulness (puppy) along with her ability to flow (cruise) into the realm of her down-to-earth adult responsibilities (disembarking on dry land). She hadn't realized how split she had become. It had never occurred to her to try to blend her soulful, fun, playful self into her work and obligations with her mother.

A few weeks later, Olivia shared with me that she was making progress blending playfulness into her work mode in little ways that were making a big difference. For example, she began playing upbeat music on the way to the office. She placed a framed photo of her dog on her desk. And when she visits her mother, she brings games (they both love Scrabble) and shifts gears from drill sergeant mode to enjoyment mode.

Wham-Bam Dream Interpretation Formula

Inspirations never go for long engagements; they demand immediate marriage to action.

BRENDAN FRANCIS

Let's face it, sometimes you have time for a luxurious dream interpretation session, and sometimes (probably more often than not) you will need a *drive-through* formula to get you through a hustle-bustle day. The Wham-Bam formula is for those moments when you are on the go and need a dream interpretation "quickie."

Wham-Bam Dream Interpretation

1. Briefly write down your dream in your dream journal.

2. As if your dream were a movie, give it a title. Go with the first thing that comes to you. For example, Olivia's title for her dream was *Not Without My Dog!*

3. Give your dream a subtitle. For example, Olivia's subtitle was *Stay in Cruise Control . . . Even On Dry Land.*

   You can learn a lot from the title and subtitle of your dreams. Immediately, the intelligence of your subconscious mind gets to work to help you identify the core essence of your dream's message.

4. Consider the possibility that everyone and everything in your dream is you. For example, in Olivia's dream, the puppy represented her innocence and instinctual self; her purse represented identity as it relates to responsibility and financial matters; the cruise ship represented the part of her related to her unconscious, her soul, and the part of her that knows life is meant to flow.

5. When in doubt as to what the symbol means, *become it*. For example, I asked Olivia to "become" the puppy and tell me how it felt to be her. She responded as the puppy, "I am so excited to play and explore, and to have Olivia be my playmate. But I am so sad when she forgets all about me when she gets back to dry land. I wish she would take me with her!"

With this simple Wham-Bam dream interpretation formula, you will at the very least capture the essence of the message and have more clarity about what action to take.

The Holy Trinity of Dreams: Angel, Ego, and Caveman

Once we've written our dreams down and applied the SADDLE formula (or at least the Wham-Bam formula), we now have a sense of what our dreams are telling us. However, in order to know how to Activate dreams in our waking lives, I've found it helpful to categorize them in one of three ways: Angel, Ego, or Caveman.

In my private sessions with individuals and couples, I incorporate subpersonality awareness and communication activities and have found it valuable in dreamwork as well. For example, we all have multiple *subpersonalities* (as distinct from *split personalities*), but we can narrow down these multiple subpersonalities into three primary archetypes:

- **Angel** (higher self, enlightened aspect)
- **Ego** (self-importance, personality preservation)
- **Caveman** (survival, basic needs)

Each of these archetypes has a particular point of view as it relates to how we live our lives by day, as well as how we sort through our business by night. Understanding these archetypes and the important role they play in our psyche can help us categorize dreams and understand how to Activate them in daily life.

Angel Dreams

At this point in your life, I'd bet your higher self (a.k.a. Angel) is probably not a complete mystery to you. I'm sure you've had moments where, out of the blue, a supernatural level of love, kindness, altruism, generosity, or plain ol' benevolence rushed through you and blew your mind, and maybe even the minds of those around you.

There is a devil in the best of us, and an angel in the worst of us. In other words, we all have an inner angel, no matter where we've been or what we've done.

A few years back (in "real" life) I was traveling by train with my family for my cousin's wedding. At one point we had to switch trains, which meant unloading all our ten tons of luggage. In the midst of the transition, my wheelchair-bound grandmother was sitting among the family baggage (pun intended) with my mom, dad, and sisters hovering around loading and unloading luggage. I spotted a huddle of young, homeless, punk-rocker types looking like vultures, leering at my grandmother's purse and our belongings. I walked past the hoodlums on my way to the bathroom and gave them my best Robert De Niro I'm-watching-you glare.

A few minutes later when I came out of the bathroom, I heard a scream. I looked up to see my eighty-five-year-old grandmother rolling down the sloping sidewalk! The break on her wheelchair had come off! Before she plunged headlong off the curb into the parking lot, the leader of the punkers ran toward her at the speed of light and stood in front of her to break her fall. The derelict

I so menacingly scowled at just moments before *saved my grandmother from major harm!* (Who was the angel and who was the devil in this scenario?) My family and I thanked him profusely and gave him some money. I gave him a bear hug, appreciating him for saving my grandma and for teaching me not to be so judgmental (I didn't tell him that part).

In that moment, much to everyone's astonishment, that young man's inner angel came shining through—probably as much to his surprise as it was to mine—and my family (and grandma) is forever grateful.

Aspects of a Daytime and/or Dreamtime Angel

- altruistic
- generous
- helpful
- selfless
- peaceful
- inspirational
- service-oriented
- connected to the *big* picture of why we are alive

Phrases Identified with the Inner Angel

- "Let go and let God."
- "It must be for the best."
- "Thy will be done."
- "Look at the big picture."

Telltale Signs of an Angel Dream

- flying
- dancing

- singing

- healing

- transcending death

- wisdom teaching

- swimming with dolphins or whales

- communing on a higher plane with departed loved ones

- connecting with a saint, sage, or someone you consider a high-vibrational being

Suggested Action to Take on Behalf of an Angel Dream

- Meditate on the feeling tone or message of the dream.

- Treat this dream as if it is a living, breathing entity, and allow it to continue and expand in its ability to elevate you.

- Carry the energy and/or message with you as you proceed throughout your day.

- Take action inspired by your dream.

The meaning of these dreams can give you a perspective on how to deal with challenges in your daily life, but most important, they are offering higher guidance, nudging you in the direction of your next evolutionary step (or quantum leap, as the case may be). To Activate these dreams, embody a feeling tone from the dream to elevate your consciousness, and then take the action they inspire.

Here's an example of how to work with an angel dream: Antonio was a quintessential manly man, with muscles galore and scars on his face from his youth spent in gangs. At a dream-workshop, he shared a recurring dream where his beloved deceased dog, Miss Lila, would come to him. In his dream he was always holding Miss Lila, and feeling such tremendous love. As he shared his dream, tears rolled down his creased face. We all witnessed the most beautiful softness wash over him, and we could all see that he was visibly glowing.

I told Antonio, "It seems to me that Miss Lila connects you to your angelic essence. If it were my dream, and if I wanted a quickening into the realm of happiness, love, intuition, and true healing power, then I'd look no further. What if this dream memory of holding Miss Lila is a custom-made key to heaven on earth. What if remembering and embodying this dream places you right in the center of yourself. If it were my dream, I would trust this reference point—this is the place from which to make decisions. I would carry this dream with me to Activate my higher self into my life, and my personal high road."

Working with Your Angel Dreams

1. Identify an Angel dream you've recently had, or one you recall from the past. For example, Doug dreamed of a higher being who showed him how to read people's energy; Ricardo dreamed about an incredible kiss that elevated him to a higher place of love and connection; and Cynthia dreamed she was flying.

   In your journal write about an angel dream that you recall.

   If you cannot recall an angel dream right now, then contemplate one of the exalted moments in your waking life (i.e., getting the green light to commence a project, receiving an award, your child being born, receiving a clean bill of health, the first time your beloved told you she loved you).

2. Now write down your *challenge du jour*. In other words, briefly describe the obstacle, difficulty, or problematic circumstance in your life you'd like resolved. For example, Doug was plagued with fear at the notion of asking his boss for the raise he felt entitled to. Ricardo had just gotten into a fight with his girlfriend, and Cynthia couldn't seem to get clients for her new business.

In your journal, briefly describe your *challenge du jour*.

3. Use your imagination (you may have to stretch a bit) to feel, envision, or imagine how your Angel dream (as you described in step 1) is the answer to your *challenge du jour*.

For example, by meditating on the confident feeling he received from his dream, Doug asked his boss for feedback on his recent performance. His boss praised him, which was the perfect entrée for Doug to request a raise. His boss took a few days to think about it and, in the end, agreed.

Ricardo felt elevated to a higher level of love in his kissing dream, so when he next saw his girlfriend, he was able to take that sensuality and empowerment with him to overcome feeling like a wounded puppy in her presence, and instead acted the swashbuckling hero that swept his girlfriend off her feet.

Before entering a recent networking meeting, Cynthia sat for a few minutes in her car, meditating on her flying dream and envisioning herself rising above her fears to a higher vibration. The effect it had on her, she later reported, was that she didn't have to feel needy, groveling, and insecure. "Instead," she gushed, "I felt like a magnet. People kept coming up to me asking me for my business card, wanting to know all about my new business. It was amazing."

Ego Dreams

In the New Age, metaphysical, and spiritual community, the ego gets a bum rap. Everyone wants to kill, annihilate, or at the very least suppress the evil ego. But what if the ego, as maniacal and diabolical as it can sometimes seem, has a purpose? I'm not saying that purpose is to rule the universe, sleep with everyone in town, or demand the biggest piece of the pie while everyone else starves. As human animals, we are survival oriented. What if our ego actually, in some cases, helps us survive by helping us be aware of what is appealing to other people and be loveable, likeable, impressive, and important so that we won't be tossed aside, neglected, or cast out.

In my experience, the only people I've witnessed that seem to have abolished their ego are wonderful and brilliant, and yet they tend to forget to brush their teeth, have an aversion to bathing, lose all track of time, and/or talk so strangely that their brilliance is often minimized as delusional meanderings, and in some cases they are relegated to the fringes of society. (The only exception to this rule seems to be the Tibetan monks I've met along my journey. They all seem to be very enlightened, clean, and articulate. I digress . . .)

So, we can see that even our ego has a role to play with us being (and remaining) on the planet. And if we think we are ever going to get rid of the ego by ignoring it, we are fooling ourselves. What is repressed must express, and when this happens in the realm of the ego, it isn't pretty. There are stories upon stories about spiritual teachers who claim to have no ego who, behind closed doors, seduce students, steal money, or lie and cheat in order to gain power. Pretending not to have an ego shoves it further into the closet—making it into something more threatening than it would ever have been if it were embraced in the light of day.

If we want to come to peace with the ego, I believe we need to remove the padlock from the closet, take the ego out of the shadows, and grant it a bit of space to live and breathe, do its basic job, and perhaps become redeemed. It may well be that the ego's basic job, when we are asleep and awake, is to simply help us pass inspection in the human condition. If the ego becomes redeemed, it might even become the chauffeur to our Angelic aspect and help us in the 3-D realm of humanhood get to where we need to go and do what we came here to do.

Aspects of a Daytime or Dreamtime Ego

- trying to look good or avoiding looking stupid
- bending over backward to fit in
- backbiting
- competing
- insecurity
- people-pleasing
- haughtiness
- showing off (overcompensating)
- being overly concerned about what other people think or say
- feeling nervous about status or position in life
- comparing one's body, possessions, or position to someone else's

Phrases Identified with the Ego

- "How dare you/he/she!"
- "Don't you know who I am?"
- "What do I get out of the deal?"
- "When will it be my turn?"

Telltale Signs of an Ego Dream

- being naked in public
- being on stage but forgetting your lines
- being publicly honored or publicly humiliated
- being at school, trying to make the grade, or running late to a class
- being at a party or public affair
- trying to get someone's affection or someone to notice you
- getting a round of applause or a standing ovation

Suggested Action to Take on Behalf of an Ego Dream

- Prepare for an upcoming event or presentation.
- Release attachment to an unsupportive relationship.
- Work to become self-accepting and self-loving.

When you awaken from an Ego dream, you can surmise that your ego in your waking life must be feeling fragile, going through a metamorphosis or change, or being overly outwardly focused. Your Ego dream often is an attempt to help you prepare for attention that is forthcoming or to see where your self-importance is disproportionately identified with a person, situation, or outcome. The opportunity available to you as you work with these kinds of dreams is that you may discover a healthier way to deal with the situation that is pressing your buttons (or perhaps learn to deactivate the button entirely!).

Kelly Clarkson, the first ever American Idol said, "Growing up, I always dreamed that I was performing at the Grammy Awards."

This is a classic Ego dream whereby the dreamer is connected to the dream the creator dreamed for them. These dreams prepare the person psychologically for fame and the pressures of performing at a high level. Miss Clarkson Activated her dream by singing every chance she could, and by taking the steps to audition for the first season of *American Idol* . . . and the rest is history.

One of my most frequently recurring Ego dreams takes place back in junior high school. The situation is always different but the recurring theme is me being ignored and shunned by my then boyfriend. I believe, because my heart (and ego) was so tender back then (it has since become a fortress—just kidding), that my first real-life taste of rejection was unbearably devastating, and I've been coming to terms with it ever since. I obviously now have lived enough life on earth to have a healthy (conscious) attitude toward rejection (my motto is "rejection is God's protection"). Instead of feeling defeated when I have one of these dreams, I've learned to feel grateful, because I feel that with each dream like this, I am regaining an aspect of myself that got lost, frozen, or disassociated back then. I'm grateful that this recurring dream theme connects me with a juicy aspect of my soul and shows me that just because other people may reject me, I don't have to!

No one can make you feel inferior without your consent.
ELEANOR ROOSEVELT

Here is a completely different type of Ego dream: For years, Sage had a reoccurring dream that she and her husband were harboring a dead body in their home.

"I always woke up from this dream feeling remorse and shame, as though we'd killed something in real life."

In our session Sage was able to see the corpse was her marriage. She and her husband had grown apart. The marriage, which once was a living, thriving entity, now was fallen apart (dead). Yet there were many people who believed them to be the perfect couple. Sage and her husband continued harboring this death in their home, because their relationship was a centerpiece of both of their identities.

Sage felt trapped by the community idea even though it was false.

I reminded Sage that she had directorial input over her dream (and her life, for that matter). With that, I encouraged her to reenter her dreamscape and redirect her dream toward a more satisfying conclusion:

> We are at a lush funeral ceremony in the woods, surrounded by tall trees and flowers. We are gathered to honor and celebrate the beautiful parts of our marriage. We gently lay the body in the ground (it's a being that looks like a hybrid of him and me, wearing a white and black tuxedo, with a wedding veil over it.) We cover it with soil. We weep tears of sorrow as we release the body. We also share our favorite and most magical memories of our relationship. Together we plant flowers in the soil covering the body, creating a sanctuary where we can both go to be with the memory of what once was.

Because Sage did the dreamwork (Activation) to uncover, discover, and discard what was no longer useful, she was able to recover a precious dimension of her own creative soul.

"That dream has haunted me for years, but now I feel liberated."

Dream synchronicity alert! When I called Sage to ask for permission to discuss her dream in this book I got her answering machine and was leaving a long message about her "Corpse in the living room" dream. She picked up the receiver with a sleepy voice and said, "Hi."

I quickly apologized, "I'm so sorry . . . it sounds like I woke you from a nap!"

"No, I had just done yoga and I was lying on the living room floor in *shavasana*." Shavasana is a rest pose done at the end of a yoga class, where you lay down on the ground, face up. It is also known as "*corpse* pose."

"No way!" I was thrilled. What a beautiful confirmation—at the very least, that's what synchronicities are to me: a wink, a nudge, a hug from the universe saying "You're on the right track!"

The cherry on top is that when I asked her how she was doing in the relationship aspect of life (I knew that after her divorce she had taken quite a long time to feel, heal, and allow her new self to reveal).

She replied, "Well, I guess you haven't read my latest article in the *Topanga Messenger!*"

I sheepishly confessed I'd been so wrapped up in the writing of this book that I hadn't.

"The new article is called "Vive le Bisou!" and it is all about my new romance. It's been years since I've been really kissed. I feel so alive!"

Apparently all the work she had been doing to feel, heal, and reveal (including the dreamwork) had paid off. She'd given the past the proper burial it deserved and thus had full permission to enjoy her just desserts . . . one kiss at a time.[15]

Caveman Dreams

In the previous Portal (*E* Is for *Embodiment*) we discussed in depth the type of dreams (or nightmares) that relate to the category I call *Caveman dreams*. All the grand and glorious work of becoming the most enlightened human being you can be would be null and void in this dimension were it not for the survival of your physical vehicle (a.k.a. your body). Your inner caveman's sole focus is to keep you in the land of the living, procreating to perpetuate the race, with a shelter over your head and food in your belly. After all, what good would it be for you to be the light of the world if you can't pay your light bill?

Caveman dreams offer opportunities to rehearse creative problem solving. When you are forewarned, you are fore-armed. Your Caveman dreams may also be helping you vent out unhealthy energy, beliefs, or patterns so that you can be a suitable host for what could serve you on a higher level.

Aspects of a Daytime or Dreamtime Caveman

- fight or flight instinct
- kill or be killed instinct
- protection of self or family
- satiation of basic instincts
- sexual urge or desire

Phrases Identified with the Inner Caveman

- "I'm starving!"
- "I'm terrified!"
- "I'm horny!"
- "I'm so furious!"
- "I'd kill for that!"
- "I'm out of control!"

Telltale Signs of a Caveman Dream

- falling
- chasing or being chased
- destruction
- fighting for your life
- running for your life

- running but unable to move
- unable to speak
- stealing
- being robbed
- killing or being killed
- being abandoned
- being overpowered, outnumbered, overwhelmed
- having sex or being sexual

Suggested Action to Take on Behalf of Caveman Dreams

- Identify which of your basic needs *isn't* being met and explore ways to meet your needs (i.e., food, shelter, safety, security, etc.).
- Get more physical exercise.
- Find a healthy outlet for your anger, passion, grief, creativity, and self-expression.

I was interviewing the president of the International Association for the Study of Dreams, Robert Hoss, PhD, for my weekly web radio show. As we were talking I discovered he had done deep research in the realm of color in dreams. No coincidence, that morning I'd written in my journal the following dream:

I'm in a bank, talking to a personal banker so that I could get a safety deposit box for my late, beloved dog, Woofie's pink leash.

Since the color of the leash stood out from the rest of the dream, I thought I'd mention it to Robert to see if he had anything to say. I told him my immediate interpretation was that I was missing Woofie, and although I'd been moving through my grieving process, I was afraid I'd forget her. So, I wanted to keep her precious pink leash (my tie to her) in a safe place.

Robert Hoss's point of view was a horse of a different color (so to speak). He said, "Pink is blend of red and white. According to my research, red symbolizes unbridled passion, self-expression, and wildness (Caveman.) When you add white to the red, you tame the red, curb its enthusiasm, and rein it in (Ego.) It's interesting that you dreamed of a pink leash, because the primary function of a leash is to rein in the animal (aspect), to tame its wildness, and make it more domesticated. Where do you feel reined in?"

You could have knocked me over with a pink feather. I responded, "Everywhere! I am a rebel at heart, a wild woman who wants to run off and break out of every social norm and container there is. And yet I love the security and serenity of all those beloved containers and structures. What a cognitive dissonance I am!"

With this dream I could clearly see the dance between my Caveman and my Ego, all wrapped up in this amazing little pink leash. My dream Activation was, as I told my husband, "This year we are going to Burning Man!" (Don't worry, I won't leave you out, dear dreamer. I'll post the pictures on Facebook!)

Sex/Erotic Dreams

Is it just me, or is it getting hot in here? Thus far, in the exploration of Caveman dreams, we've explored the scary, the frightening, the challenging, and even the spooky aspects in the previous Portal. Now let's explore some of the more pleasurable aspects (a.k.a. sex dreams).

Besides our primal *urge to merge* for the purposes of propagating the species, sex dreams are a natural way to release pent-up desire that may not be appropriate to express in your waking reality, based on your moral code, societal laws, or the length of your leash. Sex dreams are the ultimate safe sex practice, as well as being a wonderful opportunity for the inner Caveman to run wild—so that you may awaken as the balanced, civilized, upstanding citizen you are.

Erotic dreams can also help to balance out unsatisfied physical attractions or longings. Sexual expression, whether in waking life or in our dreams, causes us to feel alive within our body temple, attractive or attracted, and in touch with physical expression, celebrating the miracle of being alive.

I can't count how many conversations I've had with people who feel ashamed or embarrassed of their sex dreams. I believe that is because the unedited, triple-X way of being in dreams can sometimes be vastly different from our proper, politically correct daytime self-definitions. As is the case with most dreams, they are seldom to be translated literally. So if you have a sexual encounter with your best friend, coworker, neighbor, or even a family member, don't worry that there is something wrong with you or that you secretly harbor a desire to be sexually intimate with them. We would do well to consider our sex dreams as metaphors for connecting to, integrating, or embracing the qualities we ascribe to the person in our dream with whom we are "joining."

For example, here is a correspondence I had with a client that sought me out via email about her mysterious (and frequently recurring) sex dreams:

Dear Kelly,
I'm happily married, and my husband and I have great sex—when we have it. However, I keep having these dreams where I'm fooling around with other men. Sometimes in the dreams I'm aware that I am married and judge myself for having an

affair. Sometimes in my dreams I'm not married, and other times I realize I'm married halfway through the act. All these dream escapades take place in different scenarios: One took place on a gondola ride in Venice; one took place in an ex-boyfriend's house; and one on a copy machine in an office with a coworker. The bizarre thing is that these dreams are highly sexually charged, but they rarely ever end in actual intercourse.

Sure, I'd like to have more sex with my husband (in real life and in my dreams). I don't want to cheat on him in real life and suffer the consequences that would involve. Yet I wonder what's wrong with me. Why do I keep dreaming about other men? Help!

Thank you,
Brittany

I responded:

Dear Brittany,

Ever wondered why when you say you want your cake and to eat it too, people say, "In your dreams!" That's because in your dreams you can have sex with everyone, in every position, in every exotic locale and still wake up in the morning wrapped in the stability of your monogamous marriage!

On a purely physical level, your recurring sex dreams may simply be an indication of your strong libido and a high sex drive (congratulations)—one that may not be getting fully satisfied in the physical realm. It sounds like you and your husband's libidos may not be equally matched. Don't worry. It's rare when people fall in love with someone who has an identical sexual appetite.

Look on the bright side: You are alive in your body temple and feel a great degree of sensuality coursing through you. This is a good thing! And the fact that you've found a harmless outlet for your sexual energy while maintaining your commitment to your marriage vows is wonderful. The only thing in question is your shame about your dreams. If I were you, I'd stop condemning yourself and enjoy them.

We can learn a lot about these kinds of dreams from the Senoi, a dream-based, native culture in the highlands of Malaysia. Renowned anthropologist Kilton Stewart considered the Senoi to be a highly enlightened dream tribe. The Senoi embraced love and sex in their dreams as a way to "grow the soul." In fact, when the Senoi had sexual dreams, they were taught to move toward the loving objects and enjoy them to the fullest. Don't you love the Senoi? Wait, it gets better: They were also encouraged to have orgasms in their dreams! It didn't matter who or what the dream object or person was; it could be a relative, a friend's spouse, an animal, or a doorknob (though I don't think the Senoi had doorknobs). The Senoi believed all dream images were aspects of the self that needed to be integrated and loved.

You are a multifaceted, multidimensional, multilayered, multiorgasmic being who has chosen to be monogamous. That is a noble task. Your nighttime escapades are nothing to be ashamed of. In fact, you should be quite proud of all the aspects of yourself you've been "embracing" in your dreamtime. There is no unfaithfulness or promiscuity in dreams because everyone and everything in your dream is an aspect of yourself!

In your waking life, I suggest that you take Kundalini yoga classes to learn to channel your amazing reservoir of sexual energy toward your higher chakras, and even toward healing others. Perhaps you and your husband can explore taking a dance class (tango or salsa) together to put some of this fabulous energy into action in your waking life, in a way that energizes your relationship.

I hope this helps!

Kelly

Angel, Ego, Caveman Integration Meditation

This meditation can be done anytime during the day, but tends to be most effective in the moments bookending your sleep (right before sleep and upon awakening—after you write your dreams down in your dream journal!). To reap the benefits of this meditation I recommend you access it in any of the following ways:

- Read the following in a meditative way, slowly contemplating each sentence, breathing deeply with each thought, pausing to close your eyes to take in each element that resonates with you.

- Record yourself reading the meditation (slowly, allowing plenty of pauses between the phrases). Play your recording for yourself to enjoy in a relaxed environment with your eyes closed.

- Download the mp3 of this meditation from *www .KellySullivanWalden.com/meditations*

- Create a relaxed atmosphere for yourself where you won't be interrupted.

- Keep a journal and pen nearby to write down any *aha*s or insights stimulated by the meditation.

———

Close your eyes, and take a few breaths.

Imagine that with each breath you take you are rising above your body. See, feel, or imagine that you can see yourself now, from above, sitting with eyes closed—yet you are primarily identified with the "You" that is floating above, rising higher and higher, getting a sense of what it means to

*be so light you could fly. From this place you truly under-
stand what it means to "rise above" your circumstances, to
feel your connection with "all that is," and to remember
your Angelic essence. Feel or sense your energy field expand
beyond the point where you can no longer see the distinc-
tion between where you end and the rest of the universe
begins. Allow yourself to rise higher and higher into a field
of oneness.*

*You are now aware of your connection with everyone,
everything, throughout all time and space. Become aware
of the thoughts you think in this state of being . . . the colors
you perceive . . . and the energetic tone you feel. This point of
view is available to you at all times, whether you are asleep or
awake.*

*And now, as you descend a beautiful spiral staircase, take
this wisdom and love with you as you gently lower yourself
to the level of the Ego. Feel the electricity and the joy emanating from this place. Feel magnetically drawn and irresistibly led, as you lower yourself to earth, to the place of
humanity in the three-dimensional expression. See, sense, or
feel the healthy aspects of the Ego, your awareness of your
body and your body of affairs. Begin to sense the value and
importance of your ability to perceive as an individual, to
discern your place in the world, and to understand appropriate ways to interact.*

*From this perspective you can also perceive with compas-
sion how you and other people get lost from time to time in
the realm of the Ego. See, sense, or feel the ways you relate to
a healthy and necessary sense of self-importance, self-respect,
and ambition to be the most healthy, successful, powerful expression of yourself you can become. Know that your
Ego can be a great blessing, in that it gives you awareness*

about how to navigate within a body in this wonderful three-dimensional world. Your healthy Ego is available to you whether you are awake or asleep, in your waking reality or in your dreams.

Continue down the spiral staircase to the underground lair of the Caveman aspect of you. Feel the depth and the raw power emanating from this place. Notice your curiosity and feel the magnetic appeal that draws you in and irresistibly leads you into a deeper realm of yourself.

Your inner Caveman is solely focused on your survival, your basic instincts, most primary needs, and primal urges, without which you would not be here right now. Scan through your life to get a sense of moments when your inner Caveman was in charge. Feel the exponential power of this part of you, the resilience, the resourcefulness, and the ability to make your way through adversity. Give thanks for this necessary aspect of you that is within you whether you are awake or asleep, in your waking reality or in your dreams.

Now, with these next few breaths, notice the spiral staircase you've been traveling elevating you higher, through the Ego realm, and transporting you back up to your Angelic realm. Take a few breaths here, and prepare to take the stairs (or perhaps escalator) back down into the realm of your Ego. Breathe here for a moment, then continue traveling downward back to the domain of your inner Caveman. Notice how your spiral staircase has become a figure eight.

Take a deep breath in and hold it for three seconds, then gently release it as you rise from the realm of the Caveman through the level of the Ego, all the way up to the bright light realm of your Angelic self. Now, as you fully exhale, allow your breath to be empty for three seconds. And now breathe in all the way, and take that breath with you as you spiral down along this figure eight to the level of your Ego. Continue your exhalation as you spiral down through the bottom of the figure eight to the realm of your Caveman. Exhale completely here as you behold the darkness of your Caveman's underground cave. And now as you gently breathe back in, spiral upward along your figure eight back up through the realm of your Ego, rising as you breathe all the way in, back up to the realm of your Angel, where you breathe, connecting with the brightest light once again.

Sense that as you breathe and relax, energetically traveling swiftly along this light-filled figure eight, transporting you seamlessly above to the Angelic realm, down into your Ego, and further down into your Caveman realm, and back up again with the next breath. With each breath cycle you are weaving your awareness, acceptance, and love as you integrate all aspects of you into a unified field of being.

The word integrity comes from the Latin root integer, which means "whole" as well as "a perfect condition." This breath cycle creates a self-generated state of internal unity, a state of union between the holy trinity within: Angel, Ego, and Caveman. You've just created a state that makes you magnetic to a more vibrant life experience that you can now access in your waking life and in your dreams.

Give thanks for the multidimensions of your being and the way your Angel, Ego, and Caveman reveal themselves in your waking dream as well as your sleeping dreams. Slowly begin to orient yourself back into this moment. Feeling wonderful, shifted, lifted, and transformed. Gently open your eyes, and enjoy the rest of your day or night.

Lucid Living

The ultimate dream Activation is to live lucidly. In Felix Wolf's book *The Art of Navigation,* he talks about treating life as if it were alive . . . because it is. What if life was leading the dance, and your job was to follow as gracefully as possible? What if every song on the radio was picked especially for you from a divine play list? What if every leaf on every tree knew your name? What if every person in every situation, consciously or unconsciously, was conspiring on behalf of your greatest good? Consider that it's true, life is in fact working on behalf of the fulfillment of your wildest dreams (and by wildest dreams I don't mean a new Lamborghini. I mean your full-blown enlightened magnificence.).

If you knew this was true, you wouldn't think of your life as a problem to be solved, but rather as a treasure hunt to explore. You would see yourself through the eyes of that which dreamed you. From this perspective you would walk with a sense of excited curiosity as you traveled from one enchanted moment to the next.

Here's an example: I'd never heard of *Damanhur* until out of nowhere it showed up on my radar three times in a week. When that happens, you don't have to be a dream expert to know you'd better pay attention.

In one of the instances, I was at a friend's house and glanced at his bookshelf. Of all the hundreds of books on his shelf, this single book, *Damanhur Temples of Humankind,* seemed to leap from the shelf. I dove in headfirst and learned that Damanhur is an intentional, artisan community near the Italian/Swiss border that some call a cult, and some call heaven on earth.

A few days later, I found a video on Facebook about the underground Damanhurian temples.

The next day, on my husband's birthday, we drove up the coast to visit a mysterious property in Malibu that our friend had been encouraging us to check out. Once we arrived at this majestic hilltop vista, I met the proprietress. We shook hands and I complimented her unusual bracelet and she tells me she got it from (guess) . . . Damanhur. She takes it off and *gives it to me!*

I'm blown away . . . I love lucid living! While my chills began to multiply (a sign that you are paying attention to the navigational nudges the universe is sending), she promptly told me she was a Damanhurian who happened to live part time in Italy and most of the time in Malibu. She then proceeded to tell me about a Damanhurian Past Life workshop she soon would be hosting the following weekend. "Would you like to come?"

In the intense flow of lucid living, the only appropriate response to something like that—irrespective of how bizarre it sounds—is yes! I call it *glowing with the flow.*

On the first day of the past life workshop, in a teepee hovering over the rocks in Malibu, I met a wizened Damanhurian goddess who was both ancient and childlike. She held a mysterious envelope for each of us participants that contained the full history of the past life we would be exploring over the weekend. She explained that the way the Damanhurians explore past lives is through a sophisticated matrix of technology, science, meditation, dreams, and having the equivalent of a jury of twelve that must concur based on their individual visions and dreams about the nature of each person's past life. The Damanhurians believe we all have multiple past lives . . . some wealthy, some poverty-stricken, some with great influence, some with relative obscurity, some amazing with fortune and fame, others in abject poverty, and most somewhere in between. Damanhurians don't believe in just telling people their past lives (that would be too easy.) They believe in making you work for it . . . in your dreams.

Before we left for the night we were instructed to receive a dream that would give us insight into the past life we would be exploring that weekend. I went to sleep with the Declaration/ question on my mind: "What was my past life?" That night I had the following dream:

> I'm five years old, shopping in a mall with my dad (an outing, in real life, that has never happened . . . normally that would be something I would have done with my mom). I'm holding his hand as we walk, as I am thoroughly enjoying my time with him. We leave the mall and go to the parking lot to get in the car. But when I start to get in the car he says, "You aren't coming with me now. I want you to go upstairs to your godmothers. You'll be staying with them for a while."
>
> I give my dad a gigantic hug and tell him I love him. Then, without skipping a beat, I run upstairs with joy because I can't wait to see my godmothers. I climb several flights of stairs in an industrial building. When I arrive, I'm in a huge corporate office with desks and people working diligently. In my dream my three godmothers all work together (Esther, Mary, and Anne Harriet) and I merrily run around the office, finger painting crescent moons on everyone's forehead. Even though all the employees were working, no one was upset with my playful mischief. Everyone in the office—especially my godmothers—are overjoyed at me being there.

The next day when I shared my dream in the class, the Damanhurian goddess nodded her head in approval and beamed a confirming smile—apparently I had the "right" dream that confirmed the primary theme of the life I was exploring.

I told her, "I'm glad that the theme is correct, but when I asked what the date was of my past life, I came up blank."

I later found out that this life took place, according to the Damanhurians, before there was recorded time, during a time that predates the Lemurians.

As the workshop continued, we painted our dreams and took walks while receiving more information about these aspects of who we were (a wonderful dream Activation, by the way). Throughout this experience I discovered more about who "I" was . . . I found out I was a priestess of an island in ancient times. My parents died when I was five years old and I was sent to live with priestesses (godmothers). Because of my joyous nature and "enlightened" way that I perceived death (I did not grieve, because in my mind my parents were just going somewhere else for a while), I was initiated at an early age in the healing arts. I led moon rituals (putting crescent moons on everyone's forehead) for the purpose of raising the energy and vibration of all beings.

Skepticism aside, all I know is that during this bizarre and wonderful experience, I was able to connect with an aspect of life that felt truly uplifting and energizing . . . a new dimension of my higher self, if you will. Painting the dream, walking with it, and exploring it in depth with a group fed my soul. It also gave me access to a part of myself (a part of life) that continues to give me tremendous joy, a higher view that I can call upon in my ordinary reality—especially when there is loss or things don't go according to my plans—to help me live a bit more lucidly than I might do otherwise.

When you live lucidly, you interpret life symbolically and you pay attention to the synchronicities. Lucid living also encourages you to look at your physical surroundings, your dog, your purse, and your food as metaphors that represent a larger context.

Your dog, for example, from a dream perspective represents your animal instincts. Your purse represents your relationship with finances and your perspective on abundance or affluence in your life. And your food represents the thoughts and belief systems you are feeding yourself.

When you live lucidly, you remember you have some directorial input over the way your life unfolds. If you are displeased with the unfolding of an interaction, consider the following options:

1. Look at your life circumstances as if it were a dream.
2. See the people you are interacting with as aspects of yourself.
3. Ask for the awareness of the gift or blessing (in disguise) from the interaction.
4. Redirect the scene in your mind's eye to unfold the way you would prefer.
5. Embody the feeling tone of your newly envisioned dream.
6. Act as if (to the best of your ability) the new way is, in fact, the truth of the situation.
7. Watch reality begin to wrap itself around your new experience.

For example, I was on the board of an organization a few years back and had a particularly frustrating and painful personality conflict with a woman who was a long-time board member. I tried every tool in my toolbox to resolve our issues (and I have a rather *huge* toolbox) and nothing seemed to work. No matter how many cartwheels and backflips I did, she could not be pleased. In fact, the more feverishly I tap danced to accommodate her insatiability, the worse it got.

When all else fails, practice what you preach. So I did. Through the lenses of lucid living, I decided to see the situation as if it were a dream. I saw that she was an aspect of myself (albeit a shadow—and in fairness, I'm sure I also represented her shadow). I envisioned this shadow aspect of myself angrily wanting to feel important and respected. Eventually I found *the place within myself that was this woman* (from an energetic perspective).

I felt how completely valid she was in her upset with me. My heart softened, my fists unclenched, my jaw unlocked, and I felt a genuine outpouring of love.

I can't say that we are now the best of friends and have sleepovers every weekend. However, I can say when I see her or think of her now, the sting is gone, and in its place is a warm feeling of genuine gratitude for having faced and embraced an important aspect of my own being.

Adventures in Dream Synchronicities

Another aspect to lucid living is to become aware of when your nighttime dream images pop out from behind the curtain of your daytime reality. And when you spot a dream synchronicity, act on it. For example, if someone gives you a look like your grandmother did in your dream, tell them so. *Pay attention* to what they say and to what the circumstances are communicating. Most importantly, follow where the energy leads.

For example, I dreamed about a mosaic piece of artwork, and, upon awakening simply wrote the word *MOSAIC* in my journal in big, bold letters. Later that morning I had a session with a client who was grieving the death of her son. During the session she told me, "My dear friend just dropped off the most amazing *mosaic*, a smiling photograph of my son, comprised of hundreds of tiny pictures of him."

A jolt of electricity coursed through me. I felt a nudge from beyond the vale! The recognition of this simple element from my dream was an entry point that opened the floodgates of communication with my client. I shared the *mosaic* synchronicity with her, which gave her an unexpected feeling of peace and reassurance. She in turn shared this with the rest of her family, who similarly felt their dearly departed was reaching across the vale, which lifted them—for a precious moment—out of their heartbreak, giving them a respite and the reassurance that his spirit had survived death.

As if that wasn't enough, sometimes it seems that synchronicities don't know when to stop. Later that same day, my mother called to tell me about a new condo that she and my father looked at in the pursuit of their dream to move to downtown L.A. She described it to me in detail and concluded by telling me it's called "*Mozaic* by Union Station."

"Mom . . . I think it's a sign . . . I have a good feeling about this place for you and Dad."

Programming Your Dreams

Beyond programming (or incubating) dreams to help manifest desires, I think what we are really wanting is synergy between our conscious and subconscious minds, our soul and ego, and our humanity and divinity. In my seventeen years as a certified clinical hypnotherapist, one thing I've learned is when someone gets in sync with themselves they tend to, as a by-product of their inner harmony, magnetize all manner of fortuitous circumstance into their life. And by contrast, those who simply plug their energy into manifesting yachts, mansions, and bazillions of dollars for the sheer egotistical "feather in the cap" are chaotic, miserable, and perpetually stressed. This kind of unsustainable imbalance ultimately brings diminishing returns to their health, relationships, and the sustainability of their empire.

Bernie Madoff is an extreme example of what happens when self-will runs riot. He defrauded clients to the tune of $65 billion, and in spite of the luxurious lifestyle he maintained for decades, he will spend the rest of his life in jail, his son took his life, and he created extraordinary pain and stress for thousands of people.

In order to create true success that sustains and builds over time, we can't leave the soul out of the success equation. If we truly desire to live our dream lives, our soul must come along for the ride so that we can find the nexus point between our inner Angel, Ego, and Caveman. The mantra for this work is "All hands on deck," or "No part left behind."

When you are grappling with a question or seeking to solve a problem, here are some hints about how to plug your subconscious mind into the mix to expedite the process of finding a solution:

1. In the moments before you tuck yourself into bed, write on a piece of paper or in your dream journal your question, challenge, problem, or issue at hand.

2. As you begin to drift off into dreamland, ask your dreams to help reveal the answer to your question (or the solution to your challenge). You might add, as a caveat, that you'd like some support remembering your dreams in the morning.

3. Enjoy a peaceful night sleep.

4. If you awaken in the night with a dream on your mind, take a moment to jot it down.

5. Upon awakening in the morning, record any dream and/or dream wisp in your dream journal. Remember words, phrases, images, and feelings are relevant to this process. (Review chapter 4, Portal 2—*R* Is for *Remembrance*.)

6. Review the entry you made in your dream journal the night before. Consider the possibility that your dream and/or dream wisp is an answer to your question. Review the SADDLE formula to decode the dream.

When you follow your bliss doors will open where you would not have thought there would be doors; and where there wouldn't be a door for anyone else.

JOSEPH CAMPBELL

Create a Dream Collage

In order to step up your game, as it relates to programming your dreams, one of the most wonderful things you can do is to create a dream collage that you gaze upon (or meditate on) prior to entering dreamland. Here's the drill:

1. Line up energetically with *that which dreamed you.*

2. Revisit the Declaration meditation from chapter 3, Portal 1—*D* is for *Declaration* (page 31) to get clear about what you want . . . what you really, really, really, really want . . . all the way at the core of your being (not just on the surface, ego level).

3. Create a Dream Collage by cutting images out of a magazine (or assemble a "board" online at *Pinterest.com*) that incorporates all your desires. Or you can create separate dream collages or boards for the nine different domains of your life:

   - spirit
   - health/fitness
   - relationship/family
   - work/career
   - finances
   - sex/intimacy
   - rest/recreation
   - charity/philanthropy
   - travel/bucket list

Give yourself permission to create without editing. And please don't think that you initially need to be overly spiritually mature. This is an opportunity for you to play and get your *yayas* out. By giving yourself permission to play in the sandbox of your wildest desires, with no holds barred, you might discover aspects of your desire or destiny that had never occurred to you before.

It is important that you relate to this process in a fun and playful way. Know that it is safe to swing out and envision all you've ever desired, as well as all that you never knew you desired. Once it's all out in plain view, your vein of gold will rise up like the phoenix from the ashes. This collage is not one to get attached to too soon. Think of it as a living, breathing entity in constant change. Shift this collage, add to it, and discard elements that no longer seem relevant. Tend to it; keep it fresh, organic, an up-to-the-minute reflection of your ever-changing, ever-evolving, ever-awakening, ever-activating soul.

You see things, and you say, "Why?" But I dream things that never were, and I say, "Why not?"

GEORGE BERNARD SHAW

Dream Collage Meditation

This meditation can be done anytime during the day but tends to be most effective in the moments bookending your sleep (right before sleep and upon awakening—after you write your dreams down in your dream journal!). To reap the benefits of this meditation I recommend you access it in any of the following ways:

- Read the following in a meditative way, slowly contemplating each sentence, breathing deeply with each thought, pausing to close your eyes to take in each element that resonates with you.

- Record yourself reading the meditation (slowly, allowing plenty of pauses between the phrases). Play your recording for yourself to enjoy in a relaxed environment with your eyes closed.

- Download the mp3 of this meditation from *www
  .KellySullivanWalden.com/meditations*
- Create a relaxed atmosphere for yourself where you
  won't be interrupted.
- Keep a journal and pen nearby to write down your
  *aha*s or insights stimulated by the meditation.

———

*While looking at your Dream Collage for a few moments,
take some deep breaths. As you are breathing, envision you are
taking all these dreams and desires into your heart.*

*Close your eyes and envision your heart becoming larger
and larger with each breath—so big it contains all the images
on your Dream Collage, and all that they represent.*

*With these next breaths, feel, see, or imagine there is no
longer anything outside you. From this breath forward, everything you want or need is literally within you, inside you,
digested within your blood, your sinew, and your cells.*

*With this next breath, know all your dreams and desires are
whole-heartedly integrated, incorporated, and absorbed into
the fabric of you.*

*Take a few more deep breaths to energetically shift and alter
your reference point of who you think you are. Who you used
to be a few moments ago was one who wanted so much, one
who had such great hunger, desire, and yearning for accom-
plishment, love, and proof of outward signs of success. Now,
with each breath, your orientation is becoming that of one
who already has it all. There is, at this moment, nothing outside yourself you could possibly want or need. Your relationships are thriving; your passport is full of stamps from journeys
around the world; your bills are more than paid; your family
is in great shape emotionally and physically; your sex life is*

fulfilling; your body is in the best shape it has ever been in; you make a meaningful difference in the world; your bucket list is fully checked off.

Breathe that in. Notice if there are any "yeah buts." If so, just exhale all resistance, and release it. Now, simply bask here in the fullness of your absolute contentedness with your dream life in full bloom. Describe how you feel in a single word.

This word is now your key word to Activate your dream-life . . . from the inside out.

From a place of overflowing fulfillment, bask in the questions:

"Now that I already have it all, what am I truly inspired to do in my life?"

"Now that I already have it all, what do I want to create?"

"Now that I already have it all, what action do I feel inspired to take?"

As you take this meditation into your dreamtime, make an inner agreement with yourself that upon awakening, you will take one baby step of inspired action that aligns you with this feeling or state of being.

Give thanks for all that you've just experienced and integrated, as well as for all the ways you have transformed in these brief moments. Go to sleep knowing that something wonderful is happening to you . . . and as you are lifted, all are lifted.

In a real sense all life is interrelated. All men are caught in an inescapable network of mutuality, tied in a single garment of destiny. Whatever affects one directly affects all indirectly. I can never be what I ought to be until you are what you ought to be, and you can never be what you ought to be until I am what I ought to be. This is the interrelated structure of reality.

MARTIN LUTHER KING JR.

Upon awakening . . .

1. Write down your dreams (or any snippets you are able to recall.)

2. If there is a significant image from your dream (i.e., ruby slippers, a bumblebee, etc.), then add that image to your Dream Collage as a way of telling your subconscious mind you are playing and paying attention—willing to see the ways in which this dream might be a clue to help you manifest your dream-life.

3. Allow the spirit of curiosity and adventure to accompany you through this process. Notice when images from your nighttime dreams show up in your waking life. When they do, pay attention to them, follow them, acknowledge them in the same way a detective would who is following important clues.

4. In order to gain support, share your vision and your Action steps with your Dream Mastermind Group or your dream buddy. This process will assist you in being accountable to your dreams in your waking life (more about this in chapter 7).

5. Acknowledge yourself when you inevitably see evidence of your desire/intent becoming realized.

Dancing with the Mystery

The most beautiful thing we can experience is the mysterious.
ALBERT EINSTEIN

A Chinese Zen master poured tea for his apprentice and let the tea run over the cup and spill all over the table.

In shock, the apprentice exclaimed, "Why did you do that?"

The master replied, "Your teacup is like your mind—so full of knowledge there is no room for me to teach you anything. In order to learn something new, you must empty your cup of all that you think you know. You must create a space in your mind for wisdom to be welcome."

One of the important aspects of dream Activation is your relationship with the mystery. Many of us folks in the Western world take great pride in thinking we know it all. Our favorite phrase is "I know." And our least favorite phrase is "I don't know." It just so happens that one of the prerequisites of dream mastery is your ability to be comfortable and even excited when you truly don't know what the dream's message is.

The sky will not fall if you can't immediately figure out what your dream means or what action it's nudging you to take. The only way to ensure your receptivity to the clarity you seek is if you stand poised on the edge of your evolution, maintaining a deep-seated comfort in "I don't know" consciousness. As you do this, watch as the answers come streaming in . . . sometimes one ray at a time . . . and sometimes in bursts so bright you'll need your Ray-Bans!

Practice saying "I don't know" often . . . and breathing as you do. Imagine how much further along your evolutionary edge you would be and all the wisdom you would learn and be privy to if you could simply find a pocket of deep ease within the mystery. I'm not talking about tolerating the mystery with white knuckles, but actually getting wildly excited while you celebrate and dance like a whirling dervish with the mysterious aspects of your dreams.

Upon awakening, even if you immediately think you know what your dream's message is, and its corresponding action to take in the waking world, consider you still don't know. And while remaining connected to the dream, wrapped in a warm, fuzzy blanket of delicious not knowing, breathe . . . and with joyous curiosity watch how your intuition begins to reveal insights to you. These dream insights are not born from a pre-conceived, familiar place of tried-and-true dusty knowledge from the past but from a place of *freshly minted, soul-rocking, breakthrough wisdom that has never before found a host on earth.*

Master painter Rassouli (*www.rassouli.com*) is my greatest teacher of celebrating the mystery. Rassouli says 99 percent of the time he spends painting is in "destroying the canvas." If you saw the end product of his gorgeous, heavenly paintings you would never know that beneath each gorgeous painting are layers of paint that resembles more of a crime scene than it does a window into heaven.

"As I approach a canvas," Rassouli says, "I throw paint at it, as I am murdering everything I know, all my memory, all my expectations, all my desire to be good, and to create something pleasing to people. Once I become empty enough and I am truly in a state of not knowing anything, the painting begins to emerge. Upon reflection, I am startled at the work revealed on the canvas. Most of the time I don't recall what I did because when I am at my best, I'm not there. I am a pure vessel for God to work through."

It may sound harsh, but the best-kept secret of dreamwork is being willing to *destroy* your desire to be smart and have it all make sense. In order to access true revelation, we must be willing to be *ridiculous* and stand empty before the canvas of our dreams (and our lives) as Rassouli does when he paints. True wisdom can only come when we are naked with arms open wide, dancing with life and its mystery.

By the way, if you can't tell by now, everything true about nighttime dreamwork is also true regarding waking up and living an awakened life. When we take one step toward the mystery with an open heart, it takes ten steps toward us.

Time seems to be accelerating as if we are being pulled toward an irresistible, high-powered magnet that is our most transparent, fully actualized self . . . perhaps even a new possibility for the human race. We can either fight this magnetic pull and cling ferociously to business as usual or take the quantum leap of faith into the mystery of our dreams, toward the opportunity to truly awaken.

You must not let your life run in the ordinary way; do something that nobody else has done, something that will dazzle the world. Show that God's creative principle works in you.

PARAMAHANSA YOGANANDA

Questions for Contemplation

1. Can you recall a time when your nighttime dream gave you a deliberate command (or inspiration) for you to take action on in your waking life? If so, describe it here.

2. From a place of feeling or envisioning that you are full to overflowing, describe your dream-life.

3. Describe the action(s) you will take to Activate your dream life into being.

The way I see it, there are two kinds of dreams. One is a dream that's always going to be just that . . . a dream . . . a vision that you can never really hold in your hand. Then there's a dream that's more than a dream; it's like a map—a map that you live by and follow for the rest of your days knowing that someday you're going to stand on top of that mountain holding everything you thought of right there in your hand!

ROBERT COOPER

Chapter 7

Portal 5—
M Is for *Mastermind*

A Mastermind group is a coordination of knowledge and effort, in a spirit of harmony, between two or more people, for the attainment of a definite purpose . . . It is literally true that you can succeed best and quickest by helping others to succeed.

NAPOLEON HILL

Mastermind: (v) To plan and direct (a usually complex project or activity), especially skillfully. (n) A person who originates or is primarily responsible for the execution of a particular idea, project. (n) A Mastermind group is an alliance of two or more people dedicated to a specific goal, or in support of each other to attain his or her dreams.

Dream Masterminding

In 1928 Napoleon Hill published his first book, *The Law of Success,* commissioned at the request of Andrew Carnegie. *The Law of Success* includes sixteen lessons based on more than five hundred profiles of American millionaires including such self-made giants of industry as Alexander Graham Bell, Thomas

Edison, Henry Ford, J. P. Morgan, and John D. Rockefeller. In lesson 1 of *The Law of Success,* Hill reveals the concept of the Mastermind, which he defined as "a mind that is developed through the harmonious cooperation of two or more people who ally themselves for the purpose of accomplishing any given task." His primary message about the power of synergy between like-minded individuals was, "The mastermind group makes things happen."

I weave Napoleon Hill's concept of a Mastermind group together with the construct of a dream sharing group and, voilà!, we have Dream Masterminding! In my experience, once a dream circle has been established and each participant gets to know the other members of the group on the level of their dreams, there arises a profound soul connection and thus a rooting for one another. I have nothing against typical mastermind groups; I've been in several of them myself and have derived tremendous benefit from them. However, I feel that, in the ordinary mastermind group, people sometimes show up as human *doings* as opposed to human *beings.* When dreamwork is combined with real-world masterminding, I've found the level of connection is deeper and the ability to offer and support from a holistic perspective takes place. I guarantee that if you do this, it will not only feed your soul but also three-dimensionally change your entire life's trajectory . . . and the trajectory of all those in your Dream Mastermind Group.

Famous Dream Masterminds

Two of the original dream masterminds (though I'm quite sure that's not the label they used) were America's founding fathers, John Adams and Thomas Jefferson. As mentioned in previous Portals, they were fascinated by nighttime dreams. Either in person or via letter, these visionary men shared their nighttime dreams and daytime visions with one another. In fact, the verbiage in the Declaration of Independence comes directly from their shared dreams.

Two other famous dream masterminds were Nobel Prize–winning physicist Wolfgang Pauli, a founder of quantum theory, and Carl Jung, founder of archetypal psychology. Pauli sought out Jung for psychoanalysis during what he called "the crisis of his life." This crisis, by the way, was no small thing. It was triggered by his mother's suicide; followed by his father's hasty marriage to a woman half his age; then by his rise to fame in the world of physics; then, the final straw, the dissolution of his own marriage. Within a short period of time, Jung and Pauli expanded their professional relationship to one of profound friendship. Over time, the Jung-Pauli correspondences—albeit highly criticized by the scientific community—shared dreams and synchronicities. Because of this divine collaboration, each man was able to take his individual pioneering efforts beyond the limits of where he otherwise would have gone.[16]

In 1934 Jung gave a series of lectures titled "Psychology and Alchemy" based on the dreams Pauli shared with him. These dreams provided Jung with a rich resource for his theories. On October 2, 1935, in a letter to Jung, Pauli wrote, "I am pleased that my dreams may serve some scientific purpose." And later, in a letter from 1937, Pauli wrote, "even the most modern physics also lends itself to the symbolic representation of psychic processes, even down to the last detail."

The Law of Attraction assembles all cooperative Relationships. The Vortex is literally drawing in all things necessary for the completion of every request it contains. All cooperative components are being summoned and are coming for the completion of these creations, for the answering of these questions, for the solutions to these problems.

ABRAHAM/HICKS

Creating a Dream Mastermind Group

Being a part of a Dream Mastermind Group is a wonderful and life-changing opportunity. You may find yourself being called to join such a group. However, there may not already be a gathering of dreamers like this in your geographic area. In that case, you may be inspired to organize your own. If so, congratulations!

Here are a few guidelines to support you in hosting such a gathering:

- Create a welcoming environment (i.e., light candles, put out comfortable seats or cushions for everyone to sit on, offer tea and refreshments, etc.).

- Arrange the seats or cushions in a circle or semicircle.

- After welcoming everyone, share your intent (Declaration) or reason/inspiration for beginning the group, then invite participants to do the same.

- Lead a centering meditation or prayer. If you don't feel comfortable leading a meditation, you can download and play the mp3 of the Dream Mastermind Group Opening prayer from *www.KellySullivanWalden.com/meditations*

- Invite participants to share dreams, breakthroughs, breakdowns, or insights from the week, as well as a progress report on their personal dreams they wish to manifest in their waking lives.

  - If it is the first week, invite people to share their intentions (Declarations) for being in the group.

  - If you have a small group (less than eight to ten people), then allow each participant to share in front of the group.

- If it is a larger group, then in order to save time, encourage paired sharing.

- Typically there won't be enough time for everyone to share every dream they recall. Allow approximately five minutes for dream sharing per person.

- If the person sharing the dream is open for feedback, allow the people who have insight to offer their perspective (two to three minutes each).

- Create a closing ritual for the conclusion of each gathering. For example, invite the participants to close their eyes and, from a place of gratitude, inwardly acknowledge themselves, their dream buddy, and the entire group for sharing their dreams and daytime desires . . . and for being a part of a transformational experience. You can also download and play the mp3 of the Dream Mastermind Group Closing prayer from *www.KellySullivanWalden.com /meditations*

Dream Sharing Etiquette

Our dreams are like diamonds—besides being extremely valuable, each dream contains innumerable facets. That's why getting feedback on your nighttime dreams from a dream buddy or from your Dream Mastermind Group can be exponentially powerful.

In a Dream Mastermind Group, based on where each person is sitting, how they are feeling, and the state of mind they happen to be in, they will hear, see, and refract a different facet of light from the dream being shared. Within this space there exists the potential to experience a 360-degree dream-sharing experience. In order to gain maximum value from dream sharing, I've found it helpful to keep the following guidelines in mind.

Dream Reporting

Because dream recall connects the dreamer to the multidimensionality of the dreaming mind, there is a phenomenon that can happen with dream reporting whereby one can lose all sense of time. In other words, even the most considerate dream reporter can literally prattle on for a half hour while thinking they are sharing a brief thirty-second synopsis. Meanwhile the people on the receiving end of the dream saga struggle internally to maintain caring and compassionate listening.

(I can't help but relate this phenomenon to the passengers aboard the slapstick comedy *Airplane!*, who invent unique ways to kill themselves throughout the movie when forced to sit next to one of the two romantic leads who tell of their self-involved epic tale. With this in mind, do your best to err on the side of brevity in sharing your dreams.)

In other words, "A synopsis is bliss!"

No doubt you're familiar with REM. I'm not referring to the '80s rock band but the rapid eye movement phase of sleep when dreams are the most vivid (in most adults it occupies ninety to twenty minutes of a night's sleep, or about 20 to 25 percent of total sleep). Inspired by REM, I've coined the term *RDM*, which stands for rapid *dream* movement. RDM is a way of sharing and receiving dream insight in a relatively expeditious manner. To practice RDM, with your dream buddy or in your dream mastermind, keep the following in mind:

- **Share One Dream at a Time:** Sometimes the telling of one dream leads to the memory of another, and another, and another . . .like an endless string of pearls. If you can recall more than one dream at a time, this is *fantastic!* However, in order not to burn out the person on the receiving end of your dream report, check in with them to ensure they have the bandwidth to hear another dream.

- **Give It a Movie Title:** Imagine your dream is a movie and ask yourself, "What is the title of this movie? And what's the subtitle?" For example: *The Misplaced Soliloquy—King Richard Won't Wait; Barking Dog in the Backyard—Better Feed Him Quick;* or *Flying Through the Banyan Trees—Windy Trunks Feel Like Home.* Don't get too fancy with your dream titles. Go with the "first thought" method. The purpose of giving your dreams a title (and/or subtitle) is that it makes them memorable, reference-able, and often gives you a bull's-eye clue as to the message the dream is communicating.

- **Just the Facts, Ma'am:** Share the play-by-play of the events of the dream (i.e., "The dog was hungry and barking for me to let him in. I locked the door and threw a steak out in the back yard. I was happy the dog was now contained within the safety of my backyard.") Extreme dream details are why God created dream journals, Dream-Life Coaches, and dream therapists. Think of your dream journal as the first and best place to track every minute dream detail so that you can share the broad strokes for your dream buddy and/or Dream Mastermind Group.

- **Find the Feeling:** Identify the feeling tone or emotion of the dream (read more about this in chapter 5, Portal 3—*E* Is for *Embodiment*). In essence, the feeling or primary energy of the dream is like gold, in that it often contains the most primary aspect of the dream's message.

- **Your Synopsis:** Before allowing others to weigh in on what they think your dream is telling you, share your perspective on what you believe your dream is revealing to you.

- **Open to Receive Feedback:** If you are open to hear feedback from your dream buddy or your Dream Mastermind Group, then tell them so. If you need more time to mull over the dream within your own heart, make sure to communicate that to the group. One should not assume that just because someone shared a dream that they are open or ready to hear feedback.

Offering Feedback

When someone shares their dream with you, they stand naked standing before you (think x-ray-machine-level naked!). Their soul is exposed and the most vulnerable, fragile, brilliant, and dare I say genius aspect of them is truly laying face up on the operating table. The offering of dream feedback is not to be done cavalierly. With reverence, respect, humility, and surgical precision, listen and share with a true intent to empower the dreamer. In fact, dreamwork is all about empowerment, in the truest sense of the word. It is of extreme importance that the dreamer knows they are the ultimate authority of their dream and its interpretation. No one else but the dreamer themselves has the right to tell them definitively what their dream means.

> *Listening is the oldest and perhaps the most powerful tool of healing. When we listen, we offer with our attention an opportunity for wholeness. Our listening creates sanctuary for the homeless parts within the other person.*
>
> RACHEL NAOMI REMEN, MD

For those of us who have ears to hear, our role is to provide a safe space for the dreamer to share their dream report. Sometimes it's helpful to take notes during the dream report to track the sequence and main points of the dream. Once the dream is shared, our role is to provide feedback and reflection to support the dreamer in having their own *aha* moment. To do this, become as receptive to hearing and listening to the dream with your whole body . . . as if the dream was your very own.

A word of caution to the *empaths* of the world (you know who you are): If you are an extremely sensitive, empathic, or compassionate person, you may need to place energetic bubble of light around yourself so as to not take on someone else's dream *too* deeply. This is especially true if the dream being shared is particularly dramatic or traumatic.

Here are some guidelines for offering feedback to a fellow dreamer:

If It Were My Dream: If you preface your feedback with the statement "If it were my dream . . ." you aren't pointing an authoritative finger at someone, but you are revealing your own associations, hunches, and insights. For example, someone recently asked for my feedback on a dream about an eagle that made direct eye contact with her. I responded, "If it were my dream, I might see the eagle as a message to keep my attention on a higher plane, to acclimate to a higher vantage point, so when it's time for to come down to earth, I could do so with clarity, precision, efficiency, and intent. To me, the eye contact suggests an important part of my "eye" (I-dentity) being revealed. How does that feel? What does that bring up for you?"

She responded with an *aha* light in her eyes and a strong series of head nods.

Dream Decoding: Write out the dream as suggested in the SADDLE dream interpretation formula (see chapter 6, Portal 4—*A* Is for *Activation*, page 166). As a reminder, SADDLE stands for *symbol, association, dream dictionary, life,* and *emotion.* Once you have heard the dream report, interview the dreamer about the meaning of each symbol, how it relates to their life, and the way they felt about it in the dream. This process will shed light on the issues in the dreamer's life. For example, you might ask them, "How did you feel when the eagle looked at you? What or who did the eagle remind you of in your waking life?" Once you've completed your dream interview, share your insights with the dreamer about what you think their dream is expressing.

Actively Listen: I find people appreciate it when you truly listen to their dream report, and pause to hear what your feedback stimulates in them (i.e., "What does my sharing bring up for you?"). In fact, your active listening can be defined as absorbing the dream with all your senses, as if it truly were your own dream. This can be the most valuable aspect of the dream-sharing formula. True listening is a magnifying glass to help the dreamer see the *aha* that had been in front of them the whole time.

Become the Symbol: I find that when I ask someone about their dream and they are truly puzzled by what its bizarre symbols mean, I'll ask them to *become* the symbol. For example, Tameka dreamed of a tall building collapsing and had no earthly idea what it meant. I asked if she would be willing to *become* the building and answer the following questions:

Kelly: "What does it feel like to be the building?"

Tameka: "Someone pushed me. I'm off-balance. I'm scared because I'm about to collapse."

Kelly: "As the building, what do you want?"

Tameka: "To get all these people out of me!"

Kelly: "What do you like most about being the building?"

Tameka: "Most of the time I feel tall and strong and that I can hold everyone up."

Kelly: "What do you like least about being the building?"

Tameka:" I'm stiff, rigid, and I don't feel free to move around because I'm always carrying everyone"

Kelly: "If you could have it your way, what would you like to see happen?"

Tameka: "I'd like everyone out of me . . . a little alone time to feel the relief of having space to myself. Then I'd like some renovations . . . a new foundation and more structural support so I can relax. Oh, yes . . . whoever takes up residence in me, I want them to carry a high vibration. I only want people in me who bring something to the party, so I don't always have to do all the work to hold everyone's lives together."

Dream Alchemy: If your dream buddy shares a nightmare with you, ask them if they think/feel it is a Rehearsal Dream or a Venting Dream (see pages 107–13). Support the dreamer in discovering the "gift" of the dream/nightmare. If you and/ or the dreamer are unable to immediately see the gift, the message, or the opportunity of the dream, ask the dreamer how they would redirect the dream to bring it to a more favorable/empowering conclusion. You will gain a glimpse into the dream's gift based on what the dreamer says about their dream redirection.

For example, Sara said, "In my dream, instead of my car falling off the edge of the rocky mountain road, I would prefer the road to be wider, better paved, and not so perilous. I'd also be driving slower, steadier, and paying more attention to the road I'm on instead of being distracted as I plot how to get further up the mountain!"

From this dream redirection Sara could see that her ambition (drive) has self-destructive tendencies, and she was being advised to shift gears in order to find a more manageable, sustainable way of navigating her career path.

Nighttime Dreams as Fuel for Daytime Desires: The best dream buddies and Dream Mastermind Groups are great not only at helping each other interpret nighttime dreams, but also in seeing how nighttime dreams have a direct relationship with our process of manifesting daytime desires. Sara, mentioned previously, is an artist and was looking for new galleries to showcase her art, yet she was already overwhelmed by the showings she was currently doing. Somehow she had it wired in her mind that to be more successful, she needed more showings. In working with her dream buddy Sara recognized that sometimes more *isn't more*. Sara was relieved because she could see she was *cruisin' for a bruisin', driving* her stress level higher and higher. She realized she needed to slow down, to take better care of the accounts she had, and to incorporate a "quality, not quantity" approach.

Notice What Their Dream Brings Up for *You*: I believe dreams come from the wellspring of our soul . . . and what connects one person to their soul, on some level, connects us all to the soul of the world (thank you to *The Alchemist* by Paulo Coelho). When you encounter someone's dream, ask yourself, "What does this dream bring up for me?" "Why am I hearing this now?" "How is this dream a gift/message for me, too?" If you have your own aha moment, by all means, share it with the dreamer.

Dreams and the Hero's Journey

In working with groups of people, especially in a dream circle, I've found the Hero's Journey model to be an empowering context. In fact, over the years, I've come to use it with most everything I am involved with, from the work I do with the Dream Project students in inner-city L.A., to my communications with ambassadors and NGOs from the United Nations, to corporations working to achieve a higher vision, to coaching clients who are working on a greater level of personal dream mastery and awakening. I believe that the Hero's Journey context not only supports dreamwork and the process of becoming awakened human beings but also maps the terrain of our dreams themselves. So, what is the Hero's Journey, you ask? The Hero's Journey was resurrected by American mythologist Joseph Campbell in his book *The Hero with a Thousand Faces,* published in 1949.

The Hero's Journey, in its essence, is a model outlining the predictable stages a hero encounters on a noble quest. The Hero's Journey is also referred to in screenwriting courses as a template of an inspirational story (i.e., *Star Wars, The Matrix,* even *Groundhog Day*). I believe the reason this model has become so popular is because Joseph Campbell hit a vein of gold in his ability to lay out the soulful way humans are fundamentally wired. When we hear about an underdog who breaks through into great success, something deep within us stirs, tears form in the corners of our eyes, and we stand to cheer. We do this because unconsciously we relate to this archetypal journey on a *soul*-ular level.

In the same way our car's GPS system reduces some travel stress, we feel most confident when have a glimpse of the terrain we're on and a preview of what's around the bend. The Hero's Journey is a map of our *inner* journey, and it connects us to our soul's GPS to help us navigate our path of awakening.

By the way, this is a journey you are already on. Whether or not you know it, by virtue of the fact that you are here on earth and have chosen a three-dimensional body in which to explore this brave new world—you are a hero on a Hero's Journey. The fact that you are interested in developing a greater understanding of your dreams (in other words, your soul) means you are on a Hero's *Dream* Journey . . . and the magic has already begun!

For some, life is characterized by suffering, and for others in the same circumstances life is exhilarating. I've found the Hero's Journey to be a context that reframes what might be perceived as *inglorious* struggles, challenges, ups, and downs (which are par for the course, by the way) into something more dignified. When you remember you're a hero on a Hero's Dream Journey, there is a higher purpose unfolding in every moment of your life . . . even the most annoying and heartbreaking of situations or dreams have meaning.

The four primary stages are:

1. The Call
2. The Quest
3. The Reward
4. The Return

However, within the four stages, we can break it down in more detail with twelve stages:

1. Ordinary World
2. Call to Adventure
3. Refusal of the Call
4. Meeting the Mentor
5. Crossing the Threshold
6. Belly of the Whale
7. Tests/Allies/Enemies
8. Ordeal
9. Reward
10. Journey Back
11. Resurrection
12. Return with the Elixir

The following are an elaboration of the primary twelve stages, as well as how they tie in to dreamwork:

1. Ordinary World

This stage of the Hero's Journey relates to ordinary aspects of dreamwork, that is, your dream zone (a.k.a. your bedroom) and your habits around bedtime. For example, learning to "Feng Shui Your Dream Zone," as outlined in Portal 1, can support you in making an ordinary bedroom into a dream temple, conducive for high-frequency dreamwork.

Stage 1 is about preparation, and a great way to prepare for your journey is to make a Dream Declaration (as outlined in chapter 3, Portal 1—*D Is for Declaration*).

Contemplate the following questions: What can you change or rearrange in your dream zone to make it less chaotic and more amenable to sweet dreams? What is your personal Dream Declaration?

2. The Call to Adventure

This stage of the journey is about receiving the invitation to participate in this adventure called dream mastery (or dream awakening). There is the saying "Many are called; few answer." Consider that every night you are being called to embark on a mighty dream adventure.

In your waking life you are being called to awaken and profoundly participate in life. Do you resist these opportunities or do you seize them when they come to call? Can you recognize an invitation when it lands in your lap? When life calls, do you answer?

Contemplate the following questions: What you are being called to do? What is your relationship to opportunity when it knocks? What are the implications of your response to the call to join or create a Dream Mastermind Group? Is there someone you can call to share your dreams with?

3. Refusal of the Call

Resistance is something every dreamer and every Dream Mastermind Group experiences. We either address our reluctance unconsciously (i.e., with passive-aggressive behavior or with plain ol' rebellion), or we can address it consciously. When you shine a spotlight on resistance—just like with any good shadow—it loses its power.

Often the reason for the reluctance (or the out-and-out refusal) is simply because the call to adventure is inconvenient or in conflict with the ordinary person's agenda. Consider that the ordinary person has a mile-long list of demands for life, whereas a true hero asks only what life demands of them.

Contemplate the following questions: In what ways do you resist dreamwork? Do you think you don't have enough time or energy to contemplate your dreams? Does your morning routine take you deeper in or further away from your dreamwork? Is there any part of you that may still believe dreamwork is super-fluous, indulgent, or frivolous? Identify your resistance, shine a light on it, and allow it to dissolve so that that you may move on to the next stage.

4. Meet the Mentor

Why is it necessary to have a mentor support you through your Hero's Dream Journey?

What kind of mentor/guide/coach would be sufficient for this task? Once you identify your mentor, how will you work with them? I've found that working with a powerful mentor can make or break the Hero's Dream Journey . . . especially when times get tough, rough, or even confusing (which they inevitably do). A great mentor does the miraculous job of connecting their mentee with their own internal wisdom, guidance, confidence, and power.

There are a variety of guides and/or mentors you can choose from to support you on your noble quest. One quality a mentor should have is a familiarity with the dream realm. Some people choose a physical human guide; some choose a nonphysical saint, sage, or departed loved one; some choose a power animal; and some choose all of the above.

The late, great Carl Gustav Jung is one of my dream mentors, as is East Indian saint Anandamayi Ma. Robert Moss, highly touted dream historian, graciously mentors me from time to time. I also call upon my best friend, my sisters, and my husband to explore my personal dreams.

Contemplate the following questions: In your inner and outer world, who can you call on or look to for guidance regarding your nighttime dreams? How will you connect with your mentor? For example, if they are deceased, you might post their picture on your vision board or meditation area; if they are alive, you can set up a coaching call once a week; if they are not as available as you'd like, meditate on them before going to sleep and ask them to join you in the dreamtime.

5. Crossing the Threshold

This is the line in the sand that delineates the ordinary from the extraordinary, the mundane from the mysterious, and the awake from the asleep. Often one finds that they can't just skip across the threshold . . . because they bump right into the "Guardian" that stands between worlds. This being usually poses a difficult question or riddle to the wannabe dream hero. This is a test to see if they are worthy of passing through. By the time the hero crosses this threshold, they must do so with their whole heart, soul, and body. By struggling to pass this threshold, the wannabe hero demonstrates their commitment to becoming an actual hero, a master of the mystery of dreams.

On the level of sleep, many people have a difficult time shutting their minds off and crossing the threshold to the Land of Nod. Finding an easeful—and drug-free way—to enter sleep can be quite the riddle to solve. To outsmart the Threshold Guardian, I recommend a few drops of lavender essential oil on your pillow, mugwort balm on your temples,[17] and doing the work (as mentioned in stage 1) to declutter your dream zone.

The "riddle," as it relates to dreamwork, can often be the dream itself. Dreams are the language of the soul, and the soul speaks in pictures that, to the conscious mind, can seem absurd. One must rise to a higher level to behold the "method in the madness" and receive the true elixir of the dream.

Contemplate the following questions: What kind of ceremony can you create for yourself to mark this transition (buy a new journal, set your alarm to get up a half hour earlier to record your dreams, create a contract for yourself that you sign and date, etc.)?

6. Belly of the Whale

Now that you've crossed the threshold, from a nighttime dream perspective, this is when you close your eyes to the waking world and open your inner eyes to the topsy-turvy, *Alice in Wonderland*–esque terrain of your dreams (or more accurately, "Jonah and the Whale"–esque ocean). In some way, the belly of the whale represents every human's greatest fear: being isolated, out of control, and overpowered. To most people this "dark night of the soul" is feared as a fate worse than death. The irony is, however, once you relax into it, it's not so bad. In fact, in the dark of the belly is where the *peace that passes human understanding* can be felt. In the belly of the whale you might actually hear the voice of your own inner wisdom, and in fact, it's in the belly of the whale where the hero's initiation takes place.

On another level, the belly of the whale can be seen as the sleep that swallows us whole every night. Just as little kids scream and throw tantrums in their resistance to bedtime, once they become enveloped by the whale, they "sleep like babies."

Perhaps you've experienced a dream of isolation, rejection, or of being engulfed. Dreams of water, the ocean, or an actual whale, dolphin, or other sea creature relate to this stage of the Hero's Dream Journey. I find that people either report feeling extreme joy or extreme panic with a dream that takes place in the ocean or that features a whale. I believe these dreams, in some way, represent our relationship with the deep feminine aspect of ourselves, our relationship with our mother, our intuition/psychic abilities, our relationship with our soul, and/or the mystery of life. In time, with more dream mastery under your belt, this phase will become quite blissful—even empowering— for you are on a journey to become familiar with the largess of the magnificent being that is you.

Contemplate the following questions: Can you see the benefit of being in the belly? Have you ever experienced a dark night of the soul? If so, what benefits did you derive from the experience? What is your relationship to whales . . . to the ocean . . . to your soul . . . to the mystery of life? What is your relationship with your whale-like power?

7. Tests/Allies/Enemies

It could be said that the underlying purpose of our dreams is to regain our power and help us grow into enlightened, awakened versions of ourselves—while here on earth. If this is true, then the optimum environment for growth is a perfect storm composed of challenges, rest, and opportunities to demonstrate our new skills. If we have too much dissonance, we become weak; if we have too much softness, we become complacent.

Lucky for us, our dreams provide us with that perfect storm. Michael Bernard Beckwith says, "Pain pushes until inspiration pulls." Consider your scary, sinister, hideous dream "enemies" (just like in our waking lives) are actually allies in disguise. They have been carefully cast to haunt our Dream Theater in order to press our buttons, scare us straight, or test our mettle, so that we may find and access the core of our inner strength. The better we get at working with these kinds of dreams (chasing, fighting, running for our lives), the quicker we are able to transform them into allies.

We need our dream allies—someone to share our dreams with, people to support in our waking reality, to balance things out, to reassure us, and regenerate our confidence to take on the day. When you dream of the Dalai Lama, an angel, Mother Theresa, or your power animal, relish it and absorb the wisdom, love, and support to the last drop. Meditate on their wisdom messages throughout the day, and take the action they inspire.

Contemplate the following questions: Who are your obvious allies? Who are the most supportive people in your life? Who challenges you the most? What's your relationship to the "tests" life offers you?

8. Supreme Ordeal

You might be saying, "When does this Hero's Dream Journey get fun?" Don't worry, the reward is right around the corner . . . but first, you must *face, embrace, ace,* and *replace* the energy you most deeply F.E.A.R. As you do this, you'll transform this energy that drains your life force into that which enlivens, awakens, and puts a gale force beneath your wings. Even if you don't transform your dream creature from the black lagoon into Mary Poppins, at the very least you will have stopped resisting it. And in so doing, you will have accepted the fact that, as an infinite being, the creature from the black lagoon is one aspect of the spectrum of the eternal, never-ending being you are.

The good news is if you are able to overcome your supreme ordeal in the dream state, then you won't have to do battle with it in your waking life. This process also frees up your inner resources previously bookmarked for defense spending to now be allocated more productively in the direction of your thriving creativity, spiritual development, and your capacity to more powerfully explore the life of your dreams.

Remember that a nightmare is an unfinished dream. If you can redirect your nightmare while you are dreaming in such a way that you are exalted and empowered, then I tip my dream hat to you. If you are unable to pull off this level of lucid dreaming at this stage, don't fret. You can always do it via meditation in your waking state, or via Dream Theater (see Portal 3—*E Is for Embodiment*). For example you can envision slaying the monster, shrinking your dream nemesis to the size of a pea, pulling the plug on the person shouting at you—you get the idea.

Contemplate the following questions: What is your greatest fear? Have you ever experienced the way adversity can propel you to take a quantum leap in your life? How powerful would you feel if you transformed your fear into rocket fuel for your greatest daytime desires . . . and your full-blown awakening? What would you do, create, become if all your available energy was free to be used creatively, in a way that was truly life enhancing?

9. Reward

Okay, now the moment you've been waiting for . . . the moment you've worked so hard for . . . the moment you can finally exhale. You have properly *faced, embraced, aced,* and *replaced* your deepest fear in the supreme ordeal, so you can now claim your previously disowned power. You did this by asking the scary creature, "What gift do you have for me?" "What is your good intent?" or even "Why are you chasing me?" By doing this you have allowed what you thought was going to annihilate you to actually liberate you.

Now that aspect of power is no longer locked in a dungeon . . . it is yours . . . and it is back . . . with a vengeance (in a good way!). *B*reathe as you integrate this power, strength, beauty, wildness, fierce love, and passion back into your heart and soul. *Don't leave bed without it!*

Consider that every situation in your life and every single dream—from the seemingly benign to the over-the-top dramatic—is encoded with soul juice and power for you, should you choose to accept it. Sometimes we are able to receive the gift of the dream while we are still inside the dream. Other times we have to reconnect with our dream guide (mentor) and go after the gift in our waking state, via meditation, dream reentry, or dream theater (as described in Portal 3, page 113).

Contemplate the following questions: Can you identify the gift(s) you've received from your most recent dream(s)? How has this gift benefited you? How might this gift benefit other people? Is there a gift lingering in your dream world that you still have yet to retrieve?

10. Journey Back

Just as in stage 3 you explored the refusal of the call, in this stage you get to deal with the refusal of the return. Many heroes stop (or pause for an indefinite amount of time once they received the gift because they figure they've been through enough.

On the level of nighttime dreams, most people don't feel compelled to *have* to remember their dreams and bring them full circle. Warm and cozy in their toasty bed in the early morning hours, as the sun is gently filtering its warmth into their sleep zone, the hero has a critical choice to make. Will he or she leave their dreams on the pillow, floating aimlessly and stillborn (harsh, I know, but true) in the dreamtime? Or will the hero summon the courage to retrieve these wisps of dream brilliance and carry them back to the ordinary world? (For more information about dream recall, see Portal 2—*R* is for *Remembrance*.)

If you set yourself up properly in stage 1 by decluttering your dream zone and placing your dream journal and a pen (or your free DreamsCloud app) on your bedside table, then you are in good shape to gently make your return. Now is the time to *s-l-o-w-l-y* roll over and record your remembered dream. This represents your willingness to tiptoe your way back toward the ordinary world by remaining in the hypnagogic state—the zone between sleep and awake—while you record your dream.

Contemplate the following questions: What is your biggest challenge to dream catching in the early morning hours (i.e., being too tired, being afraid to wake up your partner, being alarmed by your alarm clock, your dog or cat jumping on your bed, rolling over and grabbing your phone to check emails, or leaping out of bed too quickly to start your day)? At your next opportunity, will you take the time to remember and record your dream(s)?

11. Resurrection

While remaining on that bridge between sleep and awake, your dream wisdom can come shining through like morning sun filtering through your bedroom drapes. Can you stand comfortably on the bridge between worlds and honor both realities as equally valid and true?

Once you are complete with recording your dream(s) in your dream journal or phone app, spend a few minutes meditating and marinating on the feeling tone or the energy of the dream. If the dream(s) didn't feel particularly emotional, then contemplate the message of the dream, its guidance, wisdom, and insight. Even if you only recall a dream wisp (i.e., a tree, red shoes, a pink leash) you keep the drawbridge down, creating access between the waking world and the enchanted world of dreams.

The mantra for this stage is "Die daily," or, if you prefer, "Be reborn daily," and the image that best describes it is the butterfly being released from its cocoon. Your dream is a butterfly . . . and so are you. By having embarked on this Hero's Dream Journey, you have allowed your former self to die. You've been swallowed by the whale, faced your deepest fear, and received the gift of exponential wisdom, and now it's time to truly embody this transformation as you face the morning with outstretched arms (or wings). *Talk about waking up on the right side of the bed!*

Contemplate the following questions: Do you see the benefit of meditating on and embodying your dream wisdom? Can you describe a dream that you recently embodied? If so, can you express the ways in which it benefited you?

12. Return with the Elixir

Dreaming tribes like the Iroquois of North America, Aborigines of Australia, and the Senoi of Malaysia believe that your dream is a gift not only for you but also for your entire tribe. In this way, these cultures truly live the philosophy, "As one is lifted, all are lifted."

When you share your dream with your dream buddy, your Dream Mastermind Group, or someone in your life, you are sharing a soul-filled gift. Remember, dreams are the language of the soul, and when a dream is shared, it can have a medicinal effect not only on the person sharing the dream but also on the person(s) receiving the dream report.

Our dreams are an elixir of spirit that can heal us like no Western medicine can. This is frequently evidenced in oncology with so many cancer patients being healed by their dreams, like Kathleen O'Keefe-Kanavos—referenced in Portal 4 (page 144). You've also heard throughout this book about life-changing contributions made by people who have heroically retrieved their dreams from their dreamscape and translated them, in the light of day, into profound breakthroughs in science, medicine, technology, and the arts.

At the very least, the sharing of dreams connects people on a soul-to-soul level, giving the sharer and the *sharee* a sense of greater connectivity to their own intuition, as well as to stronger navigational acuity. Throughout your day, every time you pause to reflect upon an image from your nighttime dream, it's as if you are drinking life-giving soul juice from your canteen filled with elixir from the extraordinary world.

Contemplate the following questions: In what ways has dream sharing benefited you? Have you had the experience of sharing a dream with someone and seen it have a positive impact on them? Have you ever received someone's dream report and been elevated, uplifted, or inspired? Can you describe how you imagine your life might unfold as you develop greater levels of dream mastery (i.e., enhanced intuition, ease, grace, enjoyment, peace, awareness, awakening)?

Five Times More

Speaking of coming home with the elixir, sometimes our dreams are elixirs from a higher plane. Like good medicine, they are truly worthy of being shared. Here's one of mine.

Keep in mind, I mostly dream in vivid Technicolor, dramatic scenes, with action galore. However, every once in a while I'll get a dream that is a distinct paternal voice telling me (sometimes yelling at me) a direct message. When this happens I can't help but think my dream guides feel that if they are too abstract I might miss the message, so they spray-paint the writing on the wall. In the case of my "Five Times More" dream, that is exactly what happened.

In my dream I heard a voice say, "See everything in your life as if it were five times more than it appears. When you see things five times more (or five times better) than you perceive them to be, then you are actually closer to seeing them as they truly are."

I got up in the morning, journaled my dream, and meditated on what that dream meant. I imagined seeing myself five times stronger, five times healthier, five times more successful, five times happier, five times wealthier, five times taller, and five times more awake. My house seemed five times more beautiful, the leaves on the trees outside my window seemed five times more vibrant, the air seemed five times sweeter, my husband was five times more handsome, and it even seemed that there was music in the air that I hadn't noticed before. With this awareness I felt a wave of peacefulness, relief, and overwhelming gratitude wash over me. I began breathing deeper, and everything seemed to glow, to have a hum to it, a warmth, and a sparkle (I wished I could see this way five times more often!).

Later that day I heard an interview with Pepper Lewis who channels Gaia on the Awakening Zone radio network. In the channeling, Gaia talked about the difference between the third and the fifth dimensions.

"In the third dimension," Gaia said in a crisp English accent (I'm paraphrasing), "we see things in black and white, good and bad, right and wrong, us and them. It's a very rigid and difficult dimension to be in. The inner critic and ego are ever present, constantly comparing and despairing. However, in the fifth dimension, there is none of that. In the fifth dimension there is an awareness of our unity with one another, connectivity, and love for and with every soul. In the fifth dimension there is a glow, an aura, a softness around every person, and everything, animate and inanimate, is seen and felt in a way that can only be described as *delicious*. It is possible to be here on earth, live productive and efficient lives, and have fifth-dimensional consciousness . . . in fact that would be the goal. When we speak of 'heaven on earth,' that's how to do it. And when we do this, we are, by far, closer to being awake than when we perceive through a third-dimensional lens."

I couldn't believe it. Gaia had just described the dimension I had been given access to that morning. I thought it curious that in my dream the voice told me to see things *five times* more than they were—not ten times, not two times, not a hundred times, but *five times more*. It makes me think that seeing things as five times more than our ordinary, mortal self perceives is a doorway to access the fifth dimension.

I can think of times from the past when I accessed the fifth dimension via meditation, prayer, dreamwork, or walking through nature. I shared this with a friend of mine who, let's just say, is fond of medicinal marijuana. He said, "It sounds like what it's like when I'm stoned. Instead of being mad at everybody, I fall in love with everybody."

I believe this is the energy people are chasing with drugs, alcohol, or any addiction . . . that natural high and *sweet* escape from the pain of the third dimension and a reconnection to a way of being in the world that is peaceful, and loving . . . like our true selves.

By yourself, with your dream buddy, or in your Dream Mastermind Group, I recommend you do this Five Times More meditation to strengthen the perception you have of yourself, your life, and of your Dream Mastermind Group. Once the meditation is complete, allow for each person to answer the following questions:

- Have you ever experienced a 5-D perspective? If so, describe it.

- Can you identify the primary difference between your 3-D and 5-D perspectives?

- In what ways can you give and receive support to make the 5-D an ordinary occurrence here on earth?

Five Times More Meditation

To reap the benefits of this meditation, I recommend you access it in any of the following ways:

- Read the following in a meditative way, slowly contemplating each sentence, breathing deeply with each thought, pausing to close your eyes to take in each element that resonates with you.

- Record yourself reading the meditation (slowly, allowing plenty of pauses between the phrases). Play your recording for yourself and/or your Dream Mastermind Group to enjoy in a relaxed environment with your eyes closed.

- Download the mp3 of this meditation from *www.KellySullivanWalden.com/meditations*

- Keep a journal and pen nearby to write down *ahas* or insights stimulated by the meditation.

Close your eyes, and take a few deep breaths. As you release each breath, let go of all attachments, all shoulds, all heaviness, and all density from the third dimension. With each inhalation, fill yourself up with your fifth-dimensional awareness, with light streaming in through the crown of your head, with love filtering into you through the rays of the sun. Like a spotlight, feel this light shining directly on you. Now you are the sun, you are radiating light through your breath, your cells, your pulse, and your heartbeat.

Feel, see, and know the glow that surrounds everyone and everything. Feel and sense that you are inseparably connected, intricately woven with the same tapestry of life as all beings.

Feel or imagine that your pulse is in sync with Mother Earth, breathing in and exhaling in rhythm with everyone on the planet, as if there were only one breath, one life, one being, and one activity . . . and you are in the center of it . . . at the center of all life.

From within this unified field, call to mind a person or situation that has been challenging you. Recognize where the stress of this situation lives in your body (i.e., in your head, in your stomach, in your heart, all over). Now with your fifth-dimensional perspective, see this person or situation as five times better than you normally do. Take deep breaths as you do this. See this person or situation as glowing, as beautiful, as a part of the oneness. Notice the difference in the way your body feels when you perceive this person from a fifth-dimensional perspective. How does this feel? What thoughts come to mind when you are seeing and feeling this way?

Perhaps you will connect with an idea about what you might do, or how you might participate differently in this situation. Know that as you see this person or situation from this fifth-dimensional perspective, the situation is already changing. Because of your awareness, you are already softening, regaining balance, and taking deeper breaths, shifting this situation for the better . . . five times better.

Give thanks for your ability to shift from the third dimension—via the bridge, known as the fourth dimension—to this higher field of love and awakened perception called the fifth dimension. Know that as you have done this, you have made and are making a difference on the planet, in your own life, and in the lives of all with whom you connect.

The Misplaced Soliloquy

Often in a typical Dream Mastermind Group or among dream buddies, dreams can support the dreamers not just with their own career goals but also with their psychological and emotional well-being as well. After a period of time working together, an interesting phenomenon takes place, wherein participants begin to dream on each other's behalf. The following is a dream I had for a friend of mine.

It's nighttime in downtown Los Angeles. The scene is romantic in a nitty-gritty kind of way. I'm on a rooftop of an artist's loft, with scaffolding all around. I see a crowd gathered on the far end of the roof, so I follow sounds of laughter and clapping to discover a Shakespearian play being performed by my friend Krista and her family. I've never seen this play in real life, but somehow I know it is a production of *Richard III*.

Playing the title role with gusto is Tom Ankeny, Krista's father, who, in real life had leukemia and had recently departed the mortal coil. Tom, playing a proud King Richard, wearing a crown with an ostentatious fur-lined coat, kept delivering his lines in an awkward way. Instead of expressing his soliloquy in private to the audience (which allows the audience to gain a glimpse into the character's deeper feelings and thoughts), he did his soliloquy when the stage was cluttered with "actors." In spite of the fact that all Krista's family members were on the stage together, talking over one another, he continued to present his "soliloquy."

As an audience member, I felt it was my duty to let Tom know he was supposed to wait until there were breaks in the conversation to insert his soliloquy. He communicated to me telepathically, "That will never happen." So he continued with his misplaced soliloquies throughout the play. I had to laugh. Instead of trying to direct the play, I decided to let go and simply enjoy this comedic, amateurish version of *Richard III*.

The following week I shared the dream with Krista (bear in mind, I had never met Tom and I knew very little about him and her relationship with him). When I told her the part about *Richard III,* she looked as if she'd seen a ghost. "My dad and I had a ritual of going to the Shakespeare festival in Portland every year together," she said. "Of all the thirty-seven plays Shakespeare wrote, *Richard III* was our favorite. My dad used to say he was Richard III because he could relate more to him than any of the Shakespearean characters. He would joke when he would leave me voicemail messages, speaking in an exaggerated Shakespearian accent, with the voice and authority of King Richard."

Krista affirmed that her dad was quite a talker—known for speaking over people and beginning an entirely new conversation while everyone else in the room was in the flow of another topic.

Krista said she had been hoping to have a dream visitation from her dad, and was sad that she, who normally has excellent dream recall, hadn't yet had one. Although she would have preferred to experience the dream herself, she was grateful, nonetheless, to have clearly been communicated with by her dad.

She said, "Perhaps the reason he couldn't enter my dream is because my head has been filled with such a cacophony since his passing. Maybe he tried to communicate with me in my dreams, but his soliloquy couldn't get through—like in the dream—he did the next best thing and dreamed through you. He must have known you would relay his message to me."

This dream gave Krista tremendous peace. She said it was confirmation for her that he still had his sense of humor and that he was still himself . . . albeit on the other side. Krista resolved to unclutter her mind to make room on the stage of her dreams for him to deliver the message directly to her next time.

Dream Transferring

Knowing others is wisdom. Knowing yourself is Enlighten-
ment. Mastering others is force. Mastering yourself is Power.

LAO-TZU

One of my favorite aspects of dreamwork is the phenomenon of transferability, where one person's dream, when shared, becomes everyone's dream. In my Dream Mastermind Groups, when someone shares a particularly vivid dream or juicy dream element, you can feel the energy of the group buzz with recognition. The principle "As one is lifted, all are lifted" is particularly present during these moments. The sharing of dreams has the potential to catapult one beyond the personal to the transpersonal, from the ego to the soul, and from three-dimensional to the multidimensional.

Dreams are a part of what Carl Jung called the Collective Unconscious. To understand the Collective Unconscious, envision a wheel on your car. Imagine every person represents an individualized spoke in the wheel, connected to a unifying hub. Our dreams take place within the hub. From this perspective, one dream is not the private property of an individual dreamer. The dream can certainly have specific meaning, benefit, and purpose for the dreamer. However, just like a child that comes from the womb of an individual mother, the child is not the property of the mother—it belongs to life. Your dreams are life's gift to you, for your direct benefit as well as a potential benefit to all who are willing and able to partake.

Suffice it to say, if you hear someone share a fantastic dream and you feel a pang of jealousy because all you've had lately are SleepWorking dreams, don't despair. My dream is your dream and your dream is my dream. So, if you want my dolphin dream, feel free to play in it. And if you don't mind, I just may climb aboard your flying dream, thank you!

Ah! This is one of the greatest benefits one can receive from participating in a Dream Mastermind Group: an endless supply of imagery, stories, entertainment, and inspiration to assist you in the creation of your dream life.

Collective Dreams

Some dreams are primarily for the individual; and some dreams are in service to the well-being or healing of a family or a community of people. And there are dreams that are so big they appear to have the potential to benefit the entire world.

My client Ellin had the following collective dream:

> I'm on an alien ship where the captain has kidnapped ten women and men from earth to perform a special ritual. We humans are instructed to pair up one man and one woman, and enter into these pods to have sex with each other. Since I am outnumbered and the aliens are armed, there is nothing I can do to resist. The man that picks me is very handsome and is called Adam. Even though we don't know each other at all he is a very tender lover. Once we are done with our sex ritual I am probed by a machine. It is uncomfortable and scary.
>
> The next thing I experience is Adam and I back on earth, on the run from the aliens. In the ritual I became pregnant . . . and because of the probing machine I am pregnant with multiples. Adam and I are partners on the quest to ensure our babies live on earth—not for some perverse alien race to use.
>
> Adam is a talented engineer and while we are the run from the aliens he builds ray guns to combat them. One such alien appears as a hydra with two heads, and when Adam shoots one of the heads, two more appear in its place. In the end we run and lose the aliens . . . barely. We know they will catch up to us and I

will be killed. My sole focus is on how I can live so my babies will be born.

I know my babies are destined for greatness, so I make arrangements for them to live after I die. I find myself connected with an underground network of powerful women. These women are married to men who run the Democratic and Republican parties, the mafia, and other political or governmental groups. They agree to be my soul sisters and to raise my children. I die in childbirth and each of these powerful women take a baby to raise as their own. Each child is groomed to take over their father's empire. As they become adults and world leaders in their own rights, they discover (through a series of dreams) they share the same birth mother, and that they are family. Because of this awareness, despite their political and national differences, peace is declared on earth.

Ellin called me for help in understanding what to do with this dream. She shared with me, "I've always been very politically active and wholeheartedly believe in my party's principles and ideologies; however, I feel that my perspective has been incredibly broadened by this dream . . . to say the least. Because of this dream I got to experience unconditionally loving each of these children/leaders with such diverse religious and political ideologies."

It's dreams like this that condition the way we think about humanity and our role in it. It's dreams like this that cause us to see the validity, and even necessity, of points of view that are 180 degrees different from our own. It's dreams like this that can shape the way we relate to humanity. It's dreams like this that, I believe, are a sign of the times.

Have you had this kind of dream? If so, share it with someone who has ears to hear its message and support you in activating it into being! The next stage in our collective evolution may be waiting until you do!

Group Dreaming

Never doubt that a small group of thoughtful, committed citizens can change the world. Indeed, it is the only thing that ever has.

MARGARET MEAD

My friend Dean was diagnosed with cancer and told by his oncologist that people who had his type of cancer had anywhere from one month to a year to live. Dean was a Jungian and had been a powerful dreamer his whole life. His dreaming community rallied around him to lend their dream support for an intensive dream weekend. During the weekend his friends shared the intent to dream in such a way as to support Dean in either (a) finding the cure for his cancer or at the very least (b) helping him to see the message of the cancer and discover the best way to work with it. During the dream circles each morning the group shared their dreams and Dean received an infusion of love and collective wisdom.

Skeptic that he is, Dean won't say definitively that it was that dream circle that healed him, but he will say that his willingness to be in the center of that much love was one of the boldest moves he's ever made and it certainly didn't hurt. By the way, it happens to be fourteen years later—Dean is not only alive and well but also thriving physically and creatively!

Needless to say, the power of a Dream Mastermind Group is exponential. The late Carlos Castaneda writes in detail about this in his book *The Art of Dreaming.* In fact he takes dreaming to a whole new level in the way he would pair people intentionally to have them lucid dream in tandem with one another.

If you and your dream group want to explore the magic of Group Dreaming, here are some basic steps:

1. Identify as specifically as possible the intent (Declaration) of the group. For example, if there is an issue, challenge, or opportunity that the group or an individual is facing, identify the outcome you'd like to receive by the conclusion of the gathering.

2. It is best if you can do an overnight experience.

3. Share a meditation together prior to bedtime that reinforces the group's intention (Declaration).

4. Upon awakening, allow time for each member to journal their dreams.

5. Assemble the group to join in a brief meditation that precedes dream sharing.

6. While each member shares their dreams (in order of who is moved to share), keep track of the common themes and symbols that could be revealing the answer, solution, or message.

7. If the person whom the group dreaming is for is inspired to speak, allow them to share their feelings, insights, gratitude, or whatever they feel moved to share.

8. Release attachment to needing to have an answer spelled out in black and white. Consider seeds of intent have been planted, and it is important to trust and honor the process.

9. Allow for a closing prayer/meditation acknowledgement ceremony.

Logic will get you from A to B. Imagination will take you everywhere.

ALBERT EINSTEIN

Questions for Contemplation

1. Regarding seeing things "five times better," what insights does this bring up in you?

2. What benefits will you derive from participating in a Dream Mastermind Group?

3. If you don't already have a group, how will you go about joining or organizing one?

   - Will you meet in person, on the phone, or via web-conferencing?

   - How often will you meet?

   - Where will you meet?

4. Describe one of your personal dreams—or one that was shared with you that would be considered a "collective dream"—that benefits the larger family of humanity.

5. How do you feel about the idea that you don't have complete ownership of your dreams, that they are meant to be shared with those who could benefit from it?

6. Describe your feelings or thoughts about the saying "As one is lifted, all are lifted."

Go confidently in the direction of your dreams! Live the life you've imagined.

HENRY DAVID THOREAU

Epilogue

After having written this book, just days before this went off to be printed I had the following dream:

> I'm leading a ceremony in a house in the woods. The atmosphere is festive and joyful. I direct everyone, "Go out into the dark woods and get lost. Once you successfully get lost (and only once you are completely lost), find your way back here to the house. Those of us who find our way back first will come look for you to help you find your way. Everyone was thrilled with this unique version of Hide and Seek. Before I set everyone off to get lost I remembered to hand out tiny flashlights (half the size of your pinky finger). "Once you are lost, use this to help you find your way back." Hooting and hollering with joy the group set off with their flashlights to go into the dark of the woods to get lost.

I woke up from this dream with a huge smile on my face. It reminded me that the process of awakening (whether through dream work or not) is truly a game that our souls joyously signed up to play together. I hope this book has served as a flashlight in the moments when you've either forgotten how magnificent you are . . . or have lost your way back home. Either way, it's been a supreme pleasure dreaming with you!

Kelly Sullivan Walden

Endnotes

1 *www.dictionary.com* All definitions that appear in this book are from this source.

2 Robert Moss, "Dreaming in the White House," *Wisdom* Magazine, http://*wisdom-magazine.com.*

3 "Episode 2: Claire's Place," *Everyday Health, www.everydayhealth .com.*

4 Bob Murray, PhD, and Alicia Fortinberry, MS, "Depression Facts and Stats," *Uplift Program,* last updated January 15, 2005, *http://www.upliftprogram.com.*

5 Tara Parker-Pope, "Learning While You Dream," April 20, 2010, *Well* blog, *The New York Times, well.blogs.nytimes.com.*

6 See the Agape International Spiritual Center website at *www.AgapeLive.com.*

7 Beth Hale, "Future Wife's Phone Number Revealed in a Dream," *Mind Power News, www.mindpowernews.com.*

8 Alex I. Askaroff, "Elias Howe: Master Engineer; a Brief History," *Home of the Sewalot Site, www.sewalot.com.*

9 Robert Moss, "Dreaming Oil," *Robert Moss: Way of the Dreamer, www.mossdreams.com.*

10 "Twelve Famous Dreams: Creativity and Famous Discoveries from Dreams," *Brilliant Dreams, www.brilliantdreams.com.*

11 "How Cameron Brought the Avatar Dream to Life," *Euronews,* February 3, 2010, *www.euronews.com.*

12 Professor Jim Horne, "The Phenomena of Human Sleep," *Loughbourough University: Loughborough Sleep Research Centre, www.lboro.ac.uk.*

13 Randi Chapnik Myers, "Problem at Work: Sleep on It," *The Globe and Mail,* February 20, 2008, *www.dreamsdocometrue.ca.*

14 Ibid.

15 Sage Knight, "Living the Dream—Part 1," October 4, 2011, *Sage Knight Literary Midwife* blog, *sageknightwrites.com;* and "Living Well: Vive Le Bisou!" March 29, 2012, *Sage Knight Literary Midwife* blog.

16 Charlene P. E. Burns, "Wolfgang Pauli, Carl Jung, and the Acausal Connecting Principle: A Case Study in Transdisciplinarity," *Metanexus*, September 1, 2011, *www .metanexus.net.*

17 See a recipe for mugwort tea online at *Annie's Remedy: www .anniesremedy.com.*

Acknowledgments

In order to bring this book from the dream realm into 3-D, I've been blessed with angels (visible and invisible) that have helped me midwife this book, one dream at a time. I'd like to celebrate, recognize, and acknowledge to high heaven the following people for their love, wisdom, and ridiculously powerful support:

Special thanks to my amazing husband, Dana Walden, for being my champion, hero, and partner in our dream life; to all the Sullivans (Jeanene, Granny, Amber, Tawni) and especially my dreamy mother, Julie Sullivan, for being my "first pass" editor and not laughing too hard at my silly spelling mystakes; my sister Shannon for being my life-long time partner in dreams and for sharing such important insights with me every time we connect. Thank you Steve Allen Media and Mara Prutting for your unending support and belief in me, and for being the best publicist in the entire universe. Jo-e Sutton for being such a brilliant friend and incredible diamond of wisdom; Devra at Dancing Word Group (and Michael) for being such a love and a *dream* of an agent; Jan and all the amazing people at Red Wheel/ Weiser for believing in me, my dreams, and my dreamwork; Victoria Collins for being an amazing bridge of love and wisdom from the other side. Thank you to my two favorite Roberts: Moss and Hoss. Robert Moss for his soulful guidance, leadership, unbelievable brilliance, and willingness to be available at a moment's notice for my bizarre dream queries; Robert Hoss for being a blessing to me by sharing his scientific dream research with me and for being the first person I've ever known to give me a satisfying answer to the question, "Why are our dreams so strange?" Bill Steirle for his insight about the Hero's Journey (and of course, thanks to Joseph Campbell for putting the Hero's Journey on the map and for making the map so accessible). Thank you to the IASD (International Association for the Study of Dreams), the entire board, staff, and members, for your incredible conferences, integrity, and ability to magnetize dreamers from around the world.

To Matt Tabrizi and Jean-Marc Emden at DreamsCloud for creating such a wonderful app to make dream recording, reflecting, and sharing so accessible and magical. All the people who contributed their dreams to me for this book, among them, Reverend Michael Beckwith, Claire Wineland, Shar Miller, Sage Knight, Krista Ankeny, Brandi, Adora Spencer, Donna M. Butler, Colleen Krause, Kathleen Kanavos, Julie Sullivan, Toby Wright, Diane Hendricks, Christy Conlin, Leslie Marcus, Rassouli, Amanda Lee, Ellin Sindell, Jenny Karns, and the amazing Nagual Woman—Gini Gentry.

A billion thank-yous to the core members of my dream circle and dream mastermind, Gypsy Racco, Ali Lyon (and baby Lyon), Jeannie Robinson, Tameka Kee, Michelle Romo, Laura Quintanilla, Jordan Ledderer, Paloma Mallman, Debbie Weisman, and Cathy Edgerton. And to the Dream Mastermind Group of my soul: Thank you Joseph Campbell, Carlos Casteneda, and Carl Jung.

About the Author

Kelly Sullivan Walden is the DreamsCloud app Dream Ambassador (*www.DreamsCloud. com*), founder of Dream-Life Coach Training and is a certified clinical hypnotherapist who has been working with people and their dreams for seventeen years. She is the author of seven books including the dream interpretation book, *I Had the Strangest Dream . . .: The Dreamer's Dictionary for the 21st Century*. She is also the author of *Dreaming Heaven, Discover Your Inner Goddess Queen, Goddess Queen Pearls of Wisdom Journal, Zone Golf, Pluck the Weeds & Plant the Seeds,* and *Dream Oracle Cards* (Summer 2013).

As a sought-after keynote speaker and popular media guest, Kelly has appeared on more than a thousand media interviews, is featured regularly on Fox News, and has been quoted in publications such as *Cosmopolitan, Elle, Brides, Seventeen, Woman's World, and Us Weekly.* Kelly can be heard on radio shows coast to coast and she reaches thousands of listeners around the world on her weekly web radio show, on DreamsCloud.com.

You can see Kelly in the documentary *Dreaming Heaven.* Kelly's dreamwork led her to the United Nations where she was inspired to create the Dream Project (*www.DreamProjectUN.org*), a nonprofit organization inspiring young people to tap into the power of their dreaming minds to solve world issues. The highlight of her career was an opportunity to speak about the Dream Project, by invitation, at the UN.

Passionate about the magical realm of dreams, Kelly considers dreams to be the most important language in which to become fluent. Known for her ability to catalyze people to awaken to their magnificence, she teaches dreamwork with a unique weave of depth, playfulness, humor, and soulfulness.

Kelly is living her dream life in enchanted Topanga Canyon, California, with her husband, film producer/director, Dana Walden, and their dogs, Shadow and Lola.

For more information visit Kelly's website (*www.KellySullivanWalden.com*), and find her on Facebook (*www.facebook.com/KellySullivanWaldenDoctorDream*), Twitter (*@kswalden*), and YouTube (*www.youtube.com/kellygq*).

To Our Readers

Conari Press, an imprint of Red Wheel/Weiser, publishes books on topics ranging from spirituality, personal growth, and relationships to women's issues, parenting, and social issues. Our mission is to publish quality books that will make a difference in people's lives—how we feel about ourselves and how we relate to one another. We value integrity, compassion, and receptivity, both in the books we publish and in the way we do business.

Our readers are our most important resource, and we appreciate your input, suggestions, and ideas about what you would like to see published.

Visit our website at *www.redwheelweiser.com* to learn about our upcoming books and free downloads, and be sure to go to *www. redwheelweiser.com/newsletter* to sign up for newsletters and exclusive offers.

You can also contact us at *info@redwheelweiser.com*.

Conari Press
an imprint of Red Wheel/Weiser, LLC
665 Third Street, Suite 400
San Francisco, CA 94107